Lean Transformations
for Small and Medium
Enterprises

Lessons Learned from Italian Businesses

Lean Transformations
for Small and Medium
Enterprises

Lessons Learned from Italian Businesses

Arnaldo Camuffo

CRC Press
Taylor & Francis Group
Boca Raton   London   New York

CRC Press is an imprint of the
Taylor & Francis Group, an **informa** business

A PRODUCTIVITY PRESS BOOK

CRC Press
Taylor & Francis Group
6000 Broken Sound Parkway NW, Suite 300
Boca Raton, FL 33487-2742

© 2017 by Taylor & Francis Group, LLC
CRC Press is an imprint of Taylor & Francis Group, an Informa business

No claim to original U.S. Government works

Printed on acid-free paper
Version Date: 20160801

International Standard Book Number-13: 978-1-4987-7363-8 (Paperback)

Library of Congress Cataloging-in-Publication Data

Names: Camuffo, Arnaldo, author.
Title: Lean transformations for small and medium enterprises : lessons learned from Italian businesses / Arnaldo Camuffo.
Description: Boca Raton, FL : CRC Press, 2017. | Includes bibliographical references and index.
Identifiers: LCCN 2016024782| ISBN 9781498773638 (pbk. : alk. paper) | ISBN 9781315397825 (ebook : alk. paper)
Subjects: LCSH: Small business--Italy--Case studies. | Organizational change--Italy--Case studies. | Reengineering (Management)--Italy--Case studies. | Lean manufacturing--Italy--Case studies.
Classification: LCC HD2346.I8 C26 2017 | DDC 658.4/063--dc23
LC record available at https://lccn.loc.gov/2016024782

Visit the Taylor & Francis Web site at
http://www.taylorandfrancis.com

and the CRC Press Web site at
http://www.crcpress.com

Printed and bound in the United States of America by
Edwards Brothers Malloy on sustainably sourced paper

To Elsa and Attilio, with love.

Contents

Acknowledgments

This book is the result of a number of research and professional projects that have had the good fortune of being able to count on the participation and collaboration of many people. In the first place, I would like to thank the researchers who, for various reasons, have contributed and participated in several research projects that I have conducted over the last few years. Among them are Fabrizio Gerli, University of Venice and Fondazione CUOA; Chiara Paolino, Catholic University of Milan and SDA Bocconi; Raffaele Secchi, SDA Bocconi and Bocconi University; and Federica de Stefano, Bocconi University. Alessandro Cordova, Francesco Querci, Aneesh Datar, and Gabriele Ceci also participated in the research projects in various capacities as research assistants at Bocconi University.

My special thanks to Bocconi University (in particular ICRIOS— Invernizzi Centre for Research on Innovation, Organization, Strategy and Entrepreneurship), SDA Bocconi (and in particular the Research Division), the University of Padua, the Ca'Foscari University of Venice, Fondazione CUOA, The Lean Enterprise Factory, and the Istituto Lean Management, in which I have worked in various capacities over the years, developing a variety of research projects on Lean Thinking in Italy.

Mario Nardi, Roberto Ronzani, Giorgio Possio, Francesco Nalini, and Tom Jackson provided helpful advice and suggestions on several occasions, encouraging the research even in the most difficult phases.

I also had the good fortune to avail myself of the cooperation and support of the Lean Enterprise Institute and the Lean Global Network—engaged in similar research projects—and in particular the comments and suggestions provided by Jim Womack, John Shook, Dan Jones, Michael Ballè, and Steve Bell as well as other colleagues from institutes affiliated with the Lean Global Network: Mark Reich, Luis and Oriol Cuatrecasas, Nestor Gavilan, Tomasz Koch, Dave Brunt, Norman Faul, Anton Gutter, Flavio Picchi, Falvio Battaglia, Marcus Chao, Boaz Tamir, Yalcin Ipbuken, Cevdet Ozdogan, Wiebe Nijdam, Matteo Consagra, Alessandro Piaccolo, and John O'Donnell. In particular, René Aernoudts of the Lean Management Institute in Holland, and Josè Ferro of the Lean Institute in Brazil contributed to the design phase.

The drafting of this work was facilitated by discussions with Italian and foreign scholars on several occasions and includes valuable contributions from Takahiro Fujimoto, University of Tokyo; John Paul MacDuffie, University of Pennsylvania; Frits Pil, University of Pittsburgh; Peter Ward, Ohio State University; Fabrizio Salvador, Instituto de Empresa; Desirée Van Dun, University of Twente; Richard Locke, Brown University; Suzanne Berger, Massachusetts Institute of Technology; Alberto Felice De Toni, University of Udine; Leonardo Buzzavo, Giuseppe Volpato, and Francesco Zirpoli, Ca' Foscari University of Venice; Monica Rossi, Milan Polytechnique; and Andrea Vinelli, University of Padua. In this same sense, also of great help was the constant contact with colleagues in the department of management and technology at Bocconi University and in particular Alfonso Gambardella, Alberto Grando, Franco Malerba, Vincenzo Perrone, Giuseppe Soda, Alessandro Minichilli, Mario Daniele Amore, Gianmario Verona, and Maurizio Zollo.

My special thanks also to Massimo Minolfi, Five-Sixty and to the territorial structures of Confindustria (the Italian employer association) and especially to Luisa Minoli, Unione Industriali Varese; Giovanni Rossitti, Confindustria Novara; Piergiuseppe Cassone, Confindustria Bergamo; Giuseppe Milan, Unindustria Treviso; Maurizio Moscatelli, Confindustria Como; Andrea Fornasier and Paolo Candotti, Unione Industriali Pordenone. Sergio Barel, Confindustria "Club dei 15," Renato Abate, Confindustria Campania and Paola Centi, Piccola Industria Confindustria provided several occasions to discuss the content of the book with small business owners, managers, and engineers around Italy.

I am especially grateful to Jacqueline Fuchs who translated and edited the manuscript.

However, my biggest thanks go to the companies that participated in the research activities, particularly those that devoted time and energy to let me understand the unfolding of their transformation.

Author

Arnaldo Camuffo, PhD, MBA, is a full professor of management at Bocconi University, where he teaches lean management and is director of ICRIOS, the Invernizzi Center for Research in Innovation, Organization, Strategy & Entrepreneurship. He previously taught at the Universities of Padova and Venice, Italy, and held visiting professor positions at the Industrial Performance Center at MIT; the School of Management of the University of Michigan, Dearborn; and the Universidad Deusto, San Sebastian.

After getting his MBA at MIT and his PhD at the University of Venice, he collaborated with the International Motor Vehicle Program at MIT and the GERPISA–Groupe d'Etudes et de Recherches Permanent sur l'Industrie et les Salariés de l'Automobile, Université d'Evry-Val d'Essonne.

As the author of several books (in English and Italian), essays, and articles in international journals, such as *Organization Science, Strategic Management Journal, Research Policy, MIT Sloan Management Review, International Journal of Operations and Production Management, Journal of Business Ethics, Industrial Relations, Industrial and Corporate Change, Industry and Innovation, European Management Review, International Journal of Human Resource Management, International Journal of Management Reviews, Entrepreneurship and Regional Development, Journal of Manufacturing Technology Management, Journal of Purchasing and Supply Management,* and *International Journal of Automotive Technology and Management,* he has consulted extensively with the most important Italian industrial groups.

He is president of Istituto Lean Management, affiliate to the Lean Global Network, scientific director of the Lean Experience Factory, and a member of the board of directors of the Lean Global Network. Has served and serves as independent director of Italian listed and nonlisted companies. His work has been widely publicized.

Introduction

This book is about lean transformations in small and medium enterprises (SMEs). It builds on two decades of research and professional experience with the application of the Lean Thinking principles and techniques in Italian SMEs.

It is dedicated to small business owners and managers who wish to grow their business and sustainably create wealth for themselves and their employees.

In many cases, the survival and prosperity of these firms depend on how they are managed. Transitioning to lean systems through lean transformation processes is an enormous opportunity available to anyone to better manage them.

The book focuses on Italian SMEs and their lean transformations. Why Italian SMEs? Why would their lean transformations be of interest outside of Italy?

The first reason is somehow romantic. As everyone knows, the historical antecedents of Lean Thinking are to be found in Venice. For centuries, the Venetian Arsenal represented a model of industrial efficiency unrivaled in Europe and in the world. The Arsenal can be considered a historical archetype of flow production in which an entire value stream, for example, relating to the assembly of a galley—all the way from raw materials to launch with supplies and crew on board—was implemented with very short lead times as most waste had been eliminated, and preparations through standardized work and careful management of materials made the process straightforward and linear. Perhaps the most emblematic episode of the "lean forerunner" in the Venetian Arsenal production was the visit of King Henry III of France, the last Valois, in 1574. As documented by a study, during this visit and especially during the dinner hosted by the Doge in honor of Henry III, a galley was assembled and launched in two hours. Historical sources do not enable identifying the exact processes used to operate with such a short throughput time, but we can certainly assume that the Arsenal's operations were characterized by an approach similar to lean, including (Conterio and Da Villa, 1995) (a) the organization of skilled workers in teams, (b) the standardization of equipment and interchangeability of ship components that were also "pre-kitted" in order to be readily usable, (c) the assembly of the vessels according to one-piece-flow once they had achieved flotation, and (d) the use of work standards and visual devices to detect or prevent mistakes in assembly.

In short, although Lean Thinking arose in Japan with Toyota 60 years ago, it finds its roots in Italy more than 500 years ago.

The second reason is that Italian SMEs are known for being able to operate successfully in mature and low-tech industries, heavily exposed to global competition. Of course, some of them benefit from the appeal and quality reputation provided by the "Made in Italy" brand in industries such as food, wine, apparel, shoes, eyewear, and fashion in general. But many others do well in other industries as well and have proven to be resilient even to the most dramatic and long recession of industrial capitalism so that the Italian manufacturing sector remains the second largest in Europe, only behind Germany. In any case, SMEs around the world might have something to learn from their Italian counterparts.

The third reason is that Italian SMEs represent the backbone not only of the Italian economy but also of Italian society. This is true in many countries around the world, but in Italy, I would say even more so. SMEs account for more than 95% of all the firms, the lion's share of GNP and 81% of employment, and are often organized into tightly coupled vertical geographical clusters with enormous welfare implications and impact on local communities. For these reasons, Italian SMEs have been widely studied and benchmarked internationally, especially by emerging and emerged countries, also for industrial policy purposes.

The fourth is that Lean Thinking has become an integral part of how Italian SMEs compete with lean transformations spreading out during the last decade. Those who had already undertaken lean transformations before the recession have proven to be better able to adapt and adjust to the new landscape. At the same time, the recession urged many more SMEs to start lean transformations accelerating a comprehensive process of transition of the Italian manufacturing sector toward Lean Thinking.

For all these reasons, the goal of this book is to distill what can be learned from Italian SMEs so that SME owners and managers, in Italy and elsewhere, are better equipped to start and sustain a lean transformation.

The book is articulated in five chapters. The first illustrates some exemplary lean transformation cases. These stories, albeit Italian, represent a sample of the typical challenges most industrial SMEs are faced with around the world and show how Lean Thinking can change the destiny of any firm. The second provides an account of the evolution of the Italian lean movement. Lean transformations do not happen in a vacuum but are embedded in a context that SME owners and managers need to understand to better craft their lean journeys. Chapter 3 illustrates the lean transformation framework—originally developed by John Shook at the Lean Enterprise Institute and now broadly used within the Lean Global Network and at the Italian Istituto Lean Management—to do two things. First, it interprets the cases illustrated in Chapter 1, explaining why those transformations were successful and the underlying logic. Second, it provides a situational and systematic approach to lean transformation in SMEs. This approach, based on five questions, allows the reduction of risk of failure in lean transformations, ensures consistency among the initiatives and alignment with the strategic goals, and facilitates monitoring the transformation progress. The fourth chapter leverages how Italian SMEs revisited the application of Lean Thinking principles and techniques to adjust to their specific context characterized by very small size, closed governance and family ownership, geographical clustering, prevalent specialization in low-tech industries with high variability, semi-craftsmanship, and strong unions. It describes the contingent factors SMEs need to consider in designing and sustaining their transformations and identifies some typical antecedents, triggering events, and paths to lean transformation.

The fifth chapter builds on the lean transformation framework and offers to SME owners and managers a guide to transformation, including the necessity to acknowledge uncertainty, how to de-risk transformations, and how to achieve operational performance improvements ensuring that they translate into financial performance improvements. This guide is grounded in the results of a recent study on the financial performance of 100 SMEs that seriously undertook a lean transformation. The findings of the study show the typical financial dynamics of SMEs' lean transformations and suggest a series of implications in terms of investment decisions and financial structure.

Ultimately, the goal of this book is to persuade SME owners and managers that they can transform their organization and put it in the best condition to navigate the ever more complex business world. This will not come easy and without pain, however. Lean transformations are risky endeavors. They require vision, patience, determination, and, sometimes, being able to capitalize on a triggering event. They require knowledge, firsthand, practical knowledge of Lean Thinking and a disciplined approach to apply and teach it throughout the organization. They also require aligning all the improvement initiatives with the company goals and to systematically monitor their impact on financial performance.

SME owners and managers can be sure that their lean transformation will entail a lot of work but also a lot of fun.

Arnaldo Camuffo

1

Little Big Lean Champions

1.1 SUPER MARIO LEAN: HOW PIETRO FIORENTINI BECAME THE TOYOTA OF ITALY

Mario Nardi is the prototype of how Italian entrepreneurs should be. Third-generation, young, international, competent, courageous, and above all fiercely dedicated to making his company, Pietro Fiorentini SpA, thrive.

Mario is all this because he made Lean Thinking not only the company's production model, but also the management system, the corporate culture, and—why not?—a philosophy of life.

Originally from Milan, which is still the heart of the company's activities, Mario started the transformation of the family business in 2000. At the time, the company was one of many medium-sized engineering companies in the province of Vicenza. Founded by his grandfather in 1938 and thanks to a curious patent relating to a control valve for LPG cars, the enterprise had experienced relative success and various ups and downs, enjoying the "long wave" of development of the legendary northeast but arriving at the end of the '90s with problems of profitability and growth.

At the generational change, Mario and his brothers, Cristiano and Paolo, took over the reins of the company and changed its course by making Lean Thinking—accurately interpreted and adopted—their guiding principle. Pietro Fiorentini's lean transformation was, to some extent, implemented by the book—so much so that, today, Pietro Fiorentini is one of the most visited companies in Italy, a destination of "journeys of hope" for entrepreneurs and managers in search of role models, a type of "place of worship" for those affected by the crisis or the inability to change who go to visit those capable of applying Lean Thinking and generating sustainable results over time.

Today, Pietro Fiorentini SpA is a leading global company that develops technology, products, and services for the distribution of natural gas with significantly superior financial performance in terms of growth, profitability, and cash generation compared to its direct competitors.

I have had the good fortune of regularly meeting Mario over the past ten years, visiting Pietro Fiorentini regularly, and speaking to the staff. From direct observation of the production model and the management system, as well as from conversations held on a number of occasions in various capacities in the *gemba* (where activities are carried out), four key elements emerged that have successfully enabled applying Lean Thinking.

The first is the entrepreneur's total support; in this case, the entrepreneur was the true creator and "engine" of the application of Lean Thinking. This support was not limited to the fact that the entrepreneur sustained and promoted the project, but was fully immersed and involved in it, becoming its initiator and incessant stimulator. Mario Nardi led the transformation of Pietro Fiorentini firsthand, for example, by taking part in all the stages and activities of the transformation process, the reformulation of the layout, the creation of manufacturing cells, and the *kaizen* weeks at the 3P sites. This was only possible because Mario himself has a profound understanding of the principles and techniques of Lean Thinking, and this knowledge comes from direct experience, gained in person through years of study (his library on Lean Thinking is impressive), through meetings and relationships with academics and national and international consultants (from Jim Womack to Chihiro Nakao to George Koenigsaecker, just to mention three *sensei*, or masters, of world stature), and through confrontation and conversations nurtured through *gemba* walks around the world. Mario has thus been the leader and *sensei* of the transformation of Pietro Fiorentini. This was possible only because he, with humility and commitment, called himself into question, investing in himself, deciding to learn the theory and practice, and putting himself in the shoes of the *deshi* (disciple).

The extensive and constant investment in knowledge of the Lean Thinking principles and techniques was the second secret of success of the lean transformation of Pietro Fiorentini. This resulted first in vast investments in training production staff and young people, especially engineers, selected with great rigor from the best Italian universities (engineering at Padua University, Polytechnic of Milan, and Bocconi University), external training courses (alternated with continuous internal training activities and experimentation in the field, in the factory, in the technical department), and more generally in offices. This cocktail of activities has allowed Lean Thinking knowledge to be disseminated systematically in all levels of the company. Fifteen years of these types of training investments have resulted in the establishment of a team of trained and motivated managers, engineers, and workers, perhaps without equal in Italy, whose energy and enthusiasm in applying Lean Thinking is also evident and palpable in simply touring the facilities.

The massive and ongoing investments in knowledge of Lean Thinking principles and techniques were then translated into the search for and acquisition of the best international expertise in the field. Thus, it was not a simple "sprinkling" of Lean Thinking in some production line with the help of some local consultant contriving to be an expert on the subject, perhaps financed by funds from business associations, but the pursuit of "real" applied knowledge. In the first place, Pietro Fiorentini gradually formed an internal unit of specialists, the *kaizen promotion office*, and in doing so did not scrimp on resources, not only in terms of quantity, but also and especially in terms of quality, even hiring at a certain point as the head of the *kaizen promotion office* a person from Boeing who was the protagonist of an imposing lean transformation process in the '90s. It is not difficult to envisage the innovative organizational, cultural, and technical scope of this operation. Transplanting Seattle to Vicenza and hearing English alongside the Vicenza dialect is just one example of the changes and innovation that the real application of Lean Thinking can bring to small businesses in Italy and everywhere else around the world.

The establishment of a strong internal *kaizen promotion office* was accompanied by a detailed and judicious use of consultants. With regard to this aspect, two elements of the experience of Pietro Fiorentini are striking: The first is the use of a number of consultants, each in their own specialization area and according to specific business needs; the second is the exclusive use of national and international excellence, namely, consultancies, large or small, that had proven content and ability to contribute to the results. Thus, in the factories of Pietro Fiorentini, which is a medium-sized enterprise operating in a mature industry, one runs the risk of encountering the best lean application skills on an international level and also running into Chihiro Nakao, a student of Taiichi Ohno and founder of Shingjiutsu; into John Black, who with Carolyn Corvi implemented the lean transformation at Boeing (which led to the famous B737 moving assembly line); into Mike Rona, former president of the Virginia Mason Medical Centre; into Tom Jackson, one of the leading expert of *hoshin kanri*; and so forth. With this approach, Pietro Fiorentini has avoided those situations typical of Lean Thinking applications in which the entrepreneur and the enterprise rely entirely on consultancies for the launch and implementation of Lean Thinking with the dual negative results of becoming dependent on external sources for continuous improvement and only achieving episodic and short-term improvements. Pietro Fiorentini has instead become a place of experimentation in which the knowledge, approaches, and methodologies of the best consulting firms are compared and hybridized with internal knowledge and with the enthusiasm and energy of the "young lions" of Pietro Fiorentini generating a unique and specific production and management model.

The third secret of success of the lean transformation led by Mario Nardi was in not considering Lean Thinking as simply a tool aimed at reducing costs, but as a management model for the sustainable generation of value. The first example of this conception of Lean Thinking is the extensive use of the scientific method in strategic planning. Pietro Fiorentini applies *hoshin kanri* (strategy deployment) structured as a portfolio of improvement projects (A3) involving the entire organizational structure. This corporate planning and control model, matured over the years, de facto replaces the traditional planning and budgeting process, reducing the risk of mistakes in strategic and managerial decisions, and releasing appropriate amounts of financial and organizational resources for improvement and growth. A second example is the strong and ever-present link between the product design, production, and supply chain aspects of the Lean Thinking application and those concerning the market, economic, and financial aspects. Also, in this case, the interpretation that Mario Nardi bestowed on Lean Thinking is profoundly different from the norm. In general, the question is posed in terms of "efficiency" or cost reduction (warehouses, personnel, space). Lean Thinking is typically conceived as a quick remedy (sometimes a "bitter medicine") to solve business problems. However, Lean Thinking used for the purpose of efficiency results in temporary and limited cost reductions and only achieves shifting problems in time. Pietro Fiorentini's approach was instead to link continuous product and process improvements to the market, to the business, asking itself through the *hoshin kanri* process if the business lines were the right ones and if the business model was appropriate, systematically evaluating the effects of decisions on the financial business dynamics to improve the net financial position and free up resources needed for investment and growth.

Finally, the fourth secret of success of "Super Mario Lean" lies in the way in which he exerts his leadership, which can be briefly summed up as a fine blend of humility, rigor, and determination. Mario's leadership is characterized by the transparency of aims and objectives, intransigence over rules and commitments, and direct operational involvement in corporate life, openness, and listening. But above all, it relies on the power of facts, on empirical evidence as the basis of decisions, and on human intelligence as a weapon to resolve them.

1.2 EZIO'S THREE DONKEYS: LEAN THINKING FOR A BETTER WORLD IN FRANDENT

Ezio Bruno is another Italian small business owner who successfully applied Lean Thinking. Determined, serious, intelligent, humble, he is dedicated to making his company a place of experimentation and a backdrop to becoming better people and improving his life and the lives of others.

His company is Frandent, a small company of 16 employees, specializing in the production of agricultural machinery, in particular, harrows, milling machines, haymaking spreaders, and rakes. When I first visited, two things struck me before entering the factory: the presence of three cute little donkeys at the entrance and the very visible power plant entirely based on renewable energy sources. Frandent was founded in 1977 at the behest of Maurilio Bruno, father of Ezio Bruno, who established the headquarters in Osasco in the province of Turin. In the best Italian tradition, Frandent initially specialized in the production of power harrows, for which Maurilio Bruno had registered an improvement patent in 1976. This propensity for product innovation continued by introducing the manufacture of hay tedders (in 1982) and other related product families. Following growth in the '80s and '90s (and the Piedmont flood of 1994), Frandent joined the Territorial Pact (local development with industrial districts), acquired land, and obtained a loan to build a new factory that was opened in 2006 through which significant innovations in the production processes were introduced. Attention to the environment through energy saving drove the choice of the lighting system in the technical offices: These so-called "light chimneys" allow taking advantage of sunlight without using electricity. Energy is supplied by means of renewable energy sources, such as solar panels on the roof and through a biomass boiler located outside the plant. Furthermore, a system of radiant floor heating provides comfortable climatic conditions for the workers in the production department. A strong sense of social responsibility has always distinguished the company. Although small in size, Frandent's production is fully integrated with product innovation: A department is dedicated to research and design specialists, and there is a host of advanced computer systems for the development of new machinery and the improvement and innovation of parts. Testing what has been developed and implemented is undertaken in a 15,000 m² testing field adjacent to the plant, which allows functional tests on prototypes. Highly qualified operators are responsible for technological innovation and the use of robotic machines.

In 2006, Frandent decided to undertake a process of change to optimize production and increase productivity. The encounter with Lean Thinking was almost accidental. Ezio Bruno explains, "We had noticed that one of our suppliers who usually had long delivery times was decidedly improving in this regard. Investigating the reason for this change, we discovered the supplier was applying lean and seeing how its processes worked better... it was love at first sight! We started with some experiments and then relied on a consulting firm to start introducing lean production in our plant too." Thus, love at first sight, an intuition derived from the ability to observe the improvement of a supplier's performance, a supplier who, in turn, had learned the principles and techniques of Lean Thinking from SKF (one of the first multinationals to introduce Lean Thinking in Italy, in the '90s). Subsequently, he read some books and started to experiment with "flow" production.

Ezio Bruno realized early on that the key issue in the transformation was not the introduction of new techniques, but for collaborators, family members, technicians, and workers to metabolize a different approach, a new way of thinking, even before production.

As Ezio Bruno states, "The hardest thing was to convince the workers to change their way of working. If people are used to doing one thing at a given time, it is difficult to make them understand that in changing you can improve it." If we add to this that Lean Thinking requires organization by cross-functional teams as opposed to the individualism typical of the way most Italian businesses work, then the difficulty in changing becomes clear. In this regard, Frandent's owner continues, "Teams have been difficult to implement because people are used to working in their own shells and ask, 'Why do I have to work for another area that up to now has not been part of my responsibilities?' In addition, it can be difficult at times to identify a leader: If there is no natural leader, then constant work is needed to train someone." The concept of teamwork is now the basis of Frandent's organizational model and a pillar of improving productivity and competitiveness in recent years.

Here, as in Pietro Fiorentini, while changing the work in the technical department and shop floor, the first step in the transformation was to train people. And also here, the key point was the direct involvement of the entrepreneur, as a student and participant in improvement projects to make it clear to everyone that the whole company should aim at improving and that it must be done seriously. Thus, Ezio Bruno participated directly in all the *kaizen projects*, not only contributing in person to improving productivity but also setting an example and emitting a clear signal of his determination.

From the technical point of view, the transformation began with the value stream mapping of power harrows, a strategic product that at the time accounted for more than 70% of turnover. Through this, the main waste was identified that contributed to holding back business productivity, including very long lead times, long machine setup times, equipment and materials that were distant from work stations, and overflowing warehouses. The adoption of the principles of Lean Thinking led to drafting a future value stream map and an improvement plan based on *kaizen weeks* aimed at eliminating waste—and this without intensifying work, working longer hours or making anyone redundant.

The main changes introduced concerned the layout, moving toward flow production, the robotization of carpentry work, the adoption of the 5S technique and visual warehouse management to give an order to useful materials and discard the useless, the introduction of *kanban* and the milk run method (*mizusumashi*), creating spaces and equipment (e.g., containers) in such a way so as to have the materials when needed, and the introduction of continuous flow work cells in the welding and assembly stages.

However, Ezio Bruno, in the most authentic adoption of the Lean Thinking principles, did not stop there, and Frandent also started to change the upstream supply chain, pursuing flow integration (a pull system based on supermarkets and FIFO lanes) with major suppliers.

Ezio Bruno also promoted a quality culture across several dimensions. First, quality in the processes: Some phases of the reorganization enabled the implementation of reliable processes to ensure the safety and ergonomics of operators. This was achieved through the use of *trystorming*, that is, immediately testing the ideas of change (an example is welding, moving from manual to automated and testing and simulating the change); the introduction of standardized work by eliminating, combining, rearranging, and simplifying tasks; and through the introduction of *poka yoke* (mistake proofing) so that as a defect emerges during production, immediate action is taken to avoid repeating the mistake.

Second, quality is reflected in the relentless development of problem-solving skills with team leaders and supervisors actively engaged in teaching CEDAC (or Ishikawa) as a tool to investigate and solve problems.

Perhaps the most original aspect of Frandent's adoption of Lean Thinking—when considering the small size of the company—is applying the logic of value and improvement in commercial and marketing activities. Increasing productivity in production but remaining inefficient or unable to improve in other areas of the business is a typical problem in many firms, especially smaller ones and particularly those with a strong technical and product culture.

Frandent's reorganization in this area began with the sales office, where Ezio introduced a visual management system of workloads to level activities based on two variables: resources and activities (establishing standard times for each macro activity). In this way, many typical commercial processes, ranging from order management to customer support to technical assistance, were streamlined. This resulted in eliminating non–value adding activities, a clearer organizational structure, and a reduction in customer order lead times as well as the reduction of stress and overtime coming from the standardization of processes, information sharing, and the simplification of procedures. What is more, Frandent proved that Lean Thinking can also be traded! Ezio Bruno developed a marketing plan based on the principles of Italian-ness, on productivity and quality associated with the adoption of Lean Thinking to build a positive image and reputation. Not based on abstract and rhetorical aspects but on a real voice of the customer (VOC) exercise, to build a promotional image that is personalized and consistent with the different target markets following a promotions narrative.

From here, active advertising campaigns focused on quality and territoriality characterized by slogans such as *"Erpici e buoi dei paesi tuoi"* (Harrows and oxen from your own town) and *"Gli italiani di qualità riducono i costi del tuo lavoro e aumentano la tua produzione"* (Excellent Italians reduce the cost of your work and increase your production).

When I asked about the results after five years of adopting the Lean Thinking principles and techniques, Ezio Bruno, as if nothing extraordinary had happened, calmly began to reel off the following results: the equivalent of 3 out of 11 workers dedicated to carrying out different activities (e.g., re-internalization of the blasting activity that was previously outsourced), improvements following the elimination of non–value added work, productivity increased 2.5-fold in terms of units produced per week and 3.4-fold in terms of units per day per person, total throughput time was reduced by 80%, and ergonomics and job safety had significantly improved.

Frandent's experience is fascinating and shows that in our business world the conditions do exist to remain competitive and return to growth in a sustainable way that does not adversely affect the environment or employment.

Frandent continued adopting the lean production system throughout the recent crisis, the effects of which have been felt but in a much less dramatic way than elsewhere.

The road to improvement never ends. As Ezio Bruno states with his calm wisdom, "We can always improve."

1.3 ENRICO'S LEAN OVENS: UNOX STYLE AND TECHNOLOGY

It is often said that a company reflects the character of the entrepreneur or the top management. This is certainly true of Unox SpA and its president, Enrico Franzolin. Unox designs, manufactures, promotes, and sells professional ovens and also provides support services for their use and maintenance. Unox has revenue of approximately €70 million and employs around 250 people in the group. At first glance, Unox may seem a "typical" small Italian company. Far from it, the "diversity" of Unox has its roots in the fact that Enrico Franzolin has little of the "typical" Italian entrepreneur.

The first element of diversity is that Enrico Franzolin has a degree in chemical engineering, and this training not only constitutes the technical background that over the years Franzolin has poured into the company, giving Unox a technological imprint, but has also provided the basis for a mindset and approach oriented toward growth, management, and structured problem solving, which as we shall see are wedded to the application of the Lean Thinking principles and techniques. In the early years of his career, Enrico Franzolin was a merchant, and this experience of contact with markets and customers, together with a way of interpreting their needs (the ability to listen to the voice of the customer), has enabled Unox to gain a commercial stronghold in more than 90 countries worldwide, obtaining approximately 90% of revenues from abroad. But, above all, innate in Franzolin is an almost maniacal attention to the pursuit of perfection (the fifth principle of Lean Thinking according to Womack and Jones) and understanding the mechanisms that enable products and especially processes to function.

Perhaps this is why—in addition to the tireless work of many people over the years who have transformed the company's processes—Unox was one of the first Italian SMEs to really apply lean production and organizational methods and, above all, to assimilate the lean principles. This is almost certainly the key to the success that Unox has had in optimizing internal flows and the supply chain: Lean techniques were not "copied, cut, and pasted" from some other companies and used to solve some current problems or pursue some cost reductions in the short term. Unox's lean techniques and methods are the inevitable consequence of the principles learned, studied, revised, and adopted by the entire company and, from the outset, by the main engine of lean transformation: the entrepreneur.

But first things first. In 1999, nine years after its foundation, Unox was configured as a traditional Italian small business that had experienced relatively rapid growth thanks to the aggressive penetration of particular market niches. The company was focused more on increasing sales, leveraging the national currency devaluations, than on structuring efficient and effective business processes and was organized according to the most classic mass production approach. The production lines "churned out" (it must be said!) large batches of products that were all the same, which were warehoused in the hope that customer orders coincided with the stock, which, of course, occurred infrequently (Enrico Franzolin, narrating the details of the situation at the time, called it "useless efficiency"). In this context, while inventories grew, the commercial department was accused of being unable to forecast demand and struggled with increasingly pressing production planning demands to improve forecasts.

Coincidentally, at that time, the sales manager was Franzolin, who, tired of having to predict the future (at Unox, the story is still told of when the engineer pulled a real crystal ball out of the drawer and then read the sales forecast), began to wonder if there was another way of operating and managing that would allow responding to market demands without having the warehouses full of products (and an empty cash till) while increasing product quality and reducing overall costs: a real challenge.

In line with the "think to simplify" corporate philosophy, Unox decided not to adapt and limit itself to managing the complexities arising from this challenge (for example, relocating to developing countries to reduce labor costs or a more sophisticated forecasting system to provide more accurate data), but to remove them by acting on the logistics–production processes and on the contact with markets to make them effective.

If the "what" was clear, the answer to "how" came when Unox, starting from 2000 and driven by the enthusiasm of its chairman, became one of the first Italian small companies to apply the Lean Thinking principles, techniques, methods, and tools. First through some localized experiments with the assembly line and, since 2004, also thanks to the intervention of young Auxiell engineers (a team of consultants who have worked as partners of the company), radically affecting the transformation of internal processes and the supply chain.

The key point was learning the principles and techniques of Lean Thinking directly and in person. Here, too, as in the case of Mario Nardi and Ezio Bruno, there were no shortcuts, but direct immersion, difficult and painful study, and experimentation with the conviction that this was the most important thing to do. Fundamental in the years of transition were the lean literature studies that Enrico Franzolin undertook in person, without delegating to others the assimilation of the lean principles. A favorite anecdote that Enrico Franzolin shared with me concerns the operation–processes matrix on a page in the book *Non-Stock Production* by Shigeo Shingo (one of the "bibles" of Lean Thinking), which kept him busy entire days (a total of seven, according to Franzolin!) before being able to understand the real essence. That an entrepreneur spends entire days puzzling over a page of a book on industrial management is perhaps the best synthesis of what is meant by being committed to and able to lead a lean transformation in a small company.

Despite this great effort, Unox experienced several difficulties in transforming, particularly in translating theoretical concepts into practical applications. Changes included intervening heavily on the production setup and layout (machinery and tooling equipment), in assembly and upstream of it, redesigning the entire range of products with a design for manufacturing approach and, above all, breaking down the "monuments."

This so-called "breaking down monuments" is another symbolic metaphor and consists of making—after due consideration and with empirical evidence in hand—brave decisions, even in contradiction with others made previously (the ability to admit mistakes based on evidence). A typical example was when Enrico Franzolin had no hesitation in supporting the decision to scrap a highly automated piece of equipment (and therefore a very expensive investment) and replace it with a more flexible, less sophisticated system but that was capable of producing according to the one-piece-flow logic.

In recent years, the transformation of Unox has continued and has progressed up to reaching a high level of operational excellence and contaminating other areas of the company in a value stream logic (design, commercial, etc.) and extending this to the supply chain, involving some leading suppliers.

This involvement has primarily focused on companies in which Franzolin's entrepreneurial contribution has been extensive: Today, the Unox Group includes Metex, which supplies Unox with semifinished sheet metal in an entirely pull approach or lean synchronization, and Velex, recently established precisely to serve Unox in the electronics field and designed on lean principles; in both cases, Enrico Franzolin is directly involved in management and strategy setting.

Unox's lean transformation was so pervasive that even the company's image has been strongly influenced by the lean principles and the way in which Unox has assimilated them: The logo is only black and white, recalling the concept of essentiality and simplicity, namely, Lean Thinking values. Unox's management system, as well as the decision-making and management processes, are based on these values, at all times as a function of simplification and customer value.

All these initiatives would not have been possible if Unox had not radically transformed in terms of organizational and human capital, also significantly increasing internal competencies thanks to which the entire organization now thinks, reasons, and acts based on the "Unox way" of Lean Thinking, on principles that the employer does not compromise on: physical flow as a "conveyor" of value creation, simplification and elimination of complexity, the overall focus on processes and not on individual operations, and vertical integration (not outsourcing!) in order to maintain control over the processes while cherishing problems as a source of value (through problem-solving and continuous improvement).

1.4 THE STUBBORN *KATA* OF GIORGIO: GLOBALIZATION, JAPANESE PARTNERSHIP, AND LEAN THINKING AT SPESSO GASKETS

I met Giorgio Possio a few years ago through a mutual friend. The story of Giorgio is emblematic of how Lean Thinking can change business and personal destinies. In his case, as in the other cases narrated in this chapter, Lean Thinking has been the common denominator of personal development, business transformation, and "evangelization" in society. Looking back over his personal journey, Giorgio recently told me, "In the early '90s, I was going through a very particular and critical transition in my life: a degree in agricultural science and a masters in economics of agricultural development from UC Berkeley, over 30 years old, and with two young children, I decided to leave my career in international cooperation and development organizations to enter the small family engineering company Spesso Gaskets."

Spesso Gaskets, established in 1926 by Giorgio's grandfather with some of his relations, had a long history in the automotive industry, producing gaskets for engines, mainly for the most critical sealing, which is between the engine block and the cylinder head, the so-called "cylinder head gasket." Other important business areas in the history of the company had traditionally been the production of seal kits for engine servicing/repairs clearly focused exclusively on the aftermarket.

After the first few years, the company became an original equipment supplier of Fiat and Lancia and at the same time started serving the burgeoning aftermarket. This dual market focus—OEM and aftermarket—lasted until after the war when the nonoriginal "sirens" aftermarket, less difficult to manage than the original parts but profitable and growing, led to no longer supplying large vehicle manufacturers.

Thus, in the early '90s, when Giorgio took over the reins, the company worked exclusively in the aftermarket. The technology content was relatively low, and the design was limited to the reverse engineering of original products. There was no quality system, not to mention a management model. Management was based on the "non-structured paternalism" of the three people running the company, and employees numbered almost a hundred.

Even in the absence of specific skills, Giorgio only needed a few months to realize that with the increasing and ongoing socioeconomic and market changes, the company would not go very far even if the profits in those years were still good. Giorgio was convinced of the imperative to change, but he also knew that he could not do it alone. Precisely due to their different beliefs and motivations, strategic differences with partners were gradually emerging. Giorgio thus decided to seek external "agents of change," business drivers that would enable the company to transform.

The first step he took was to re-engage, even if it required a great deal of effort and a little luck, with original equipment customers. First among these was Fiat Iveco in pursuit of the leveraging effect of a sector—car manufacturing in this case—which he considered by far the most challenging and educational for a company that wanted to learn and grow. Participation in the Assisted Growth Program of Iveco suppliers in '93 and '94, which Giorgio stubbornly wanted despite strong internal resistance also from the partners, was a fundamental turning point. For the first time, Spesso Gaskets was analyzed as a system, in this case a quality assessment system. It was the first and a very successful attempt in the context of the time to clarify the rules of the game. "I will always be grateful to Iveco for having given me this opportunity," Giorgio still affirms today. At the same time, he also became convinced of the need for Spesso Gaskets to develop more advanced technologies, products, and processes. In the mid-'90s, leading competitors—especially German—in the OEM market were far ahead. "I was firmly convinced of one thing," he recalls, "which was that also in this case, we could not do so alone... however, searching for a partner in Europe would not have brought many advantages with the likely risk of being acquired: We were direct competitors in the same territory." In automotive components in those days, North America and especially Asia were still relatively distant markets. It was possible to find a medium-to-large partner and technology leader that would not see Spesso Gaskets as a competitor but as a potential ally to globalize without significant investments in greenfield plants or acquisitions.

During this time, Giorgio began to travel systematically first in Europe and then in the United States and Japan, visiting the factories of various gasket manufacturers. It was, among other things, a time of technological transition from the fiber-based to the multilayered steel gaskets, much more complex in terms of the bill of materials and processes (up to 25 stages). At that time, Japan was far ahead of the rest of the world.

Giorgio was dazzled by his first visit to Toyota's gasket supplier Ishikawa Gasket in Japan (to the point that it became Spesso Gaskets' main commercial and technological partner). The emotional impact of his visit to

Japan was decisive for Giorgio: "I've always loved and admired the United States in many ways and also studied there for several years, but since that first visit to Japan, I have had such a feeling of harmony and the 'natural' flow of the manufacturing processes that I had no doubt that Japan was the example to follow and as quickly as possible. Today, I realize that this country, and Toyota in particular with its work philosophy, have become a central part of my life and not only professionally." In the early years, however, Giorgio had not gathered the cultural elements of Lean Thinking, almost exclusively focusing on product and process technologies that in those days were "more visible" to him. He was fascinated by some production solutions in the plants, in the layout and work organization, but only saw these as best practices, simple, clever and above all to be copied. Today, he says with a smile, "The Toyota production system was more of a slogan for me, a set of industry practices to discover and copy a little at a time... In fact, I had not understood a thing."

At that point, however, Giorgio found himself at a crossroads: To be able to pursue his dreams and inspire the company's management through what he had seen in Japan required the entire Spesso Gaskets' top management to become convinced, determined, and cohesive. Yet this was not the case. In his role as CEO, he came into conflict with some family members and in particular the chairman, his cousin. After several months of negotiations and damaging infighting, Giorgio was able to buy out the other shareholders and remain alone at the helm. At first, he felt that perhaps he had taken a step too far and that he had taken on too much responsibility, but then he reacted. As a first step, he involved his brother-in-law Gabriel Orsucci, 10 years younger and now a shareholder and managing director of Spesso Gaskets. The company continued to be a family business but with an almost absolute unity of purpose and cohesion since then.

Thus, thanks to the stubbornness of Giorgio, his tireless work and dozens of trips to Japan (his and his coworkers'), in "only" four years, Spesso Gaskets earned the trust of Ishikawa Gasket's top management, convincing them to sign a formal industrial and commercial collaboration (nonequity) agreement. As a result of this agreement, Spesso and Ishikawa in 2000 began codesigning and coproducing often highly innovative seals in the Spesso plants in Turin for world-class customers in the European market. Ishikawa worked as a true partner. Although very demanding, Ishikawa was very willing to support Spesso's process of improving and growing. Ishikawa had an "essential" structure characterized by skilled and versatile yet numerically limited managerial resources; support was initially focused on aspects of product and process technologies. As the collaboration continued, the Ishikawa mentality, however, strongly emerged in the Italian–Japanese meetings. Spesso Gaskets' management was thus systematically exposed to the principles and especially the behaviors underlying Lean Thinking. "These were very difficult to understand and digest at first," as Giorgio recalls, "to the point that diplomatic incidents were often on the verge of erupting. We resisted though, and today, in light of the facts, we are able to really appreciate the lessons learned indirectly through working with the Ishikawa Gasket engineers and managers."

In the 2000–2004 period, the company focused mainly on the engineering, industrialization, and production of new original equipment products intended for medium and heavy diesel engines. This focus was effective and enabled achieving a very high domestic market share. The result was not only revenue growth, but the improvement of business processes and people. "In this period, *jidoka* and one-piece-flow cells began to permeate some of our processes and our meetings. At the time, we didn't understand the full meaning of these terms and methods. But the learning process that was triggered was crucial for survival first and then for success. The application of *jidoka*, in particular, allowed obtaining and then maintaining qualitative product performance that had previously been unimaginable. In witness whereof," proudly confirms Gabriel Orsucci, "in 13 years of supplying millions of pieces mounted on engines, we have received only one complaint from a vehicle in circulation, and the root cause of the problem could not even be attributed with certainty to our work."

This first phase of the lean transformation of Spesso Gaskets was often characterized by a type of schizophrenic organizational dissociation. Although the improvement initiatives focused on products and processes shared with Japanese partners to produce visible results and changes, the rest of the production and support processes remained "immune" to change. Giorgio and his colleagues only thought about the technological and process aspects without transferring the principles and methods to the rest of the business system. They sensed that the potential for change at hand was huge but had no idea how to pursue it. "I confess that I often felt very alone at that stage" is how Giorgio remembers it today.

The turning point came in late 2004 and early 2005. In October–November 2004, Giorgio enrolled in the human resources training program for European entrepreneurs and managers organized in Tokyo by the EU–Japan Industrial Cooperation Centre. From that training course,

Giorgio knew he would have to speed up the transformation of Spesso Gaskets. From then on, he and his colleagues plunged even deeper into Lean Thinking, assiduously attending the World Class Manufacturing study tours with Prof. Yamashina offered by the EU–Japan Centre, and in one case, even sending a young engineer to Japan for a whole year to train him. He is now a fundamental component of the Spesso Gaskets management team. The main idea was to transform the *gemba* of Spesso Gaskets in Turin. Giorgio therefore asked the Japanese partners to assist the company in its efforts to transform radically and completely. Ishikawa Gaskets gave a hand, but the paucity of their managerial resources, coupled with language difficulties, forced Giorgio to seek further help. Ishikawa suggested that he seek the assistance of a trusted consulting firm called Noritsu Kiyokai, in Italy known as Japan Management Association Consulting (JMAC).

In short, the decisive and irreversible transformation began in 2005 even if, as in any process of change, phases of acceleration were followed by a slow-down and stagnation, in part due to the nonlinear nature of the learning process but also due to rethinking and internal resistance, perhaps not declared but actual. Giorgio particularly recalls with sadness the case of two plant directors who left the company after a relatively short period of service: "They wanted to apply a leadership style and management models that were not consistent with our lean vision. After these negative experiences, and hence for several years now, we have decided to no longer hire managers with significant prior experience but focus on the growth of young people instead, not necessarily with a high educational background but able to genuinely wed their humility and own determination of *kaizen*. Today, our team is entirely the result of internal development and is much more cohesive and collaborative than ever before. In short, a great team."

One of the elements of Giorgio's lean transformation of Spesso Gaskets that is most striking is his ability to self-reflect and self-criticize (which recalls the *hansei* process typical of Japanese culture) and which, alongside humility, is a fundamental aspect of lean leadership.

"I admit to not having been, especially in the early years, an easy entrepreneur for the consultant and my coworkers," Giorgio told me in a recent conversation. "My habit of being an authoritarian, micromanaging leader with little patience has, in many cases, constrained the spontaneous accession of my coworkers to Lean Thinking. In the first five years, I worked firsthand on all the changes and yes, getting significant results, but almost exclusively through top-down mechanisms and 'heroic' rather than supportive leadership. Alongside insufficient involvement, the biggest mistake I made in those years and, I admit, often pointed out by JMAC, was to throw myself into improvement before obtaining sufficient process stability, which is necessary to study and know them well. So not all changes took root, and the results, although very significant, did not always prove fully sustainable."

Despite Giorgio's modesty, the results were, in fact, significant: from halving the surface area of the plant in the face of significant growth in sales to containing the dramatic effects of the recession on contribution margins and maintaining employment and creating value (through product quality and innovation) for the customer.

Among the many examples of the significant applications of the Lean Thinking principles and techniques in Spesso Gaskets, two are particularly emblematic of the innovation that Lean Thinking has enabled achieving in the original equipment and aftermarket business.

In original equipment, innovation was very intense but also very selective, especially on the processes. This allowed improving performance with very low financial investment, developing and using mainly the expertise available in the company. The effects were very positive on the net financial position at a time when financial resources and, in particular, access to bank credit became more and more critical. In fact, Spesso Gaskets invested only in the development of internal capacity of new process technologies, especially by providing for the elimination and replacement of those that in corporate jargon are called "monuments" (oversized or ineffective plants or equipment) acquired in the past to streamline processes and maximize efficiency through economies of scale, which actually proved to be the most persistent enemies of the value stream—in short, a development and interior improvement process without any particular investments even in rigid ERP systems. ("Perhaps the worst of the monuments although invisible," says Giorgio.) The recent attainment of new prestigious customers in the auto industry is a symptom of the credibility and reputation that Spesso Gaskets has achieved through the adoption of the Lean Thinking principles and techniques. In the aftermarket, Spesso Gaskets focused instead on the level of customer service particularly through the vendor managed inventory (VMI), that is, assembling and sending daily seal kits depending on the inventory stock that customers communicate to constantly maintain customer stock levels in the desired range. This would not have been possible without internally applying the just-in-time approach and having consistent stock levels at the warehouse, reducing the size of assembly batches by reducing production setup times and the *kanban* system implemented with suppliers. The level of Spesso Gaskets' aftermarket customer service has long been firmly attested at nearly 100%. These results have earned Giorgio the award for best supplier of original spare parts of Iveco.

The crisis that began in the autumn of 2008 was certainly not painless for Spesso Gaskets. It broke the trend of improving financial results, which abruptly returned to the level before 2005. However, Giorgio's strength was avoiding regressing, not compromising and not questioning the Lean Thinking path undertaken. Indeed, in the years immediately following the outbreak of the crisis, Spesso Gaskets intensified the training programs to involve an increasing number of people in the company. The idea that investments in skills related to Lean Thinking are to be considered cyclical is confirmed by the fact that Spesso Gaskets also continued strengthening its lean promotion office. This allowed broadening the scope of action of the lean transformation process and extending it to product development, administration, and procurement. According to Giorgio, "Through these initiatives, knowledge has consolidated that in less visible processes waste is even higher than in manufacturing processes and that in order to flush it out and eliminate it, the application of the Lean Thinking principles and techniques is critical."

Giorgio has further developed Spesso Gaskets' lean transformation by cooperating with Mike Rother and using the Toyota Kata method, which has been very well received internally. The *kata* of improvement and that of coaching put people at their ease, he says, and most have managed to unchain creativity they did not know they had.

1.5 FRANCESCO'S COLD FUSION: MAKING CAREL GROW WITH LEAN THINKING

During one of his visits to Italy, Jim Womack asked me to show him some companies that, in my opinion, had developed serious and lasting lean transformations. I immediately suggested we visit Carel and meet Francesco Nalini, managing director of the group. Francesco, mid-30s, management engineer, Bocconi MBA, with experience at McKinsey and having risen through the ranks within Carel in the operations department, is the person who, accepting the challenge launched by Chairman Luigi Rossi Luciani and CEO Luigi Nalini (his father), successfully led Carel's lean transformation.

Carel Industries SpA is a profitable small-to-medium enterprise with revenues in excess of €200 million. It has been operating for more than 40 years in the air conditioning, refrigeration, and humidification sector, providing remote management and control systems for use in residential, industrial, and commercial applications. It was founded in 1973 as an assembler of electric cabinets for another company operating in the air conditioning sector.

After some years, it began to design and produce humidifiers for use in computer rooms or environments that require scrupulous humidity control to prevent excessively dry air generating electrostatic discharges with dramatic effects on mass storage.

In the early '80s, Carel was the first company in Europe to start designing and producing a microprocessor control system for air conditioners aimed at computing centers.

The experience gained in the field of computing centers allowed Carel to expand its range of products for various refrigeration applications and air conditioning technology focusing on electronic microprocessor controllers (this at the end of the '80s) as an alternative to electromechanical control.

In the early '90s, Carel exploited its technological edge by increasing the level of innovation of its products. In fact, in those years, a new programmable electronic control was launched, providing customers with programming software (EasyTools and its most recent evolution, 1tool). This allowed air conditioning and refrigeration technicians with good knowledge of applications but without specific computer training to quickly develop, with the help of a PC, algorithms for the control of machines and plants. The software thus created could then be installed on the Carel controller, which then became exclusive to that customer, enabling differentiation and customization with respect to competitor products, which otherwise would have been difficult given the similarity of components used in the construction of air conditioning and refrigeration appliances.

At the same time as developing control systems, Carel invested in monitoring systems, both local (within the system) and remote (via a phone line first and then via the Internet) to allow taking full advantage of the possibilities offered by microprocessor-based technology.

Carel was also one of the first companies in the industry to be certified ISO 9001 (1994).

Hitherto, this looks like a "normal" success story of Italian entrepreneurs in line with others (not as numerous as in the past, actually) whose recipe for success is product innovation and flexibility in responding to the market. In fact, the reason Carel has been able to remain competitive and continue to grow—even in difficult times, such as the last few years—is to be found in the lean transformation undertaken in 2007.

The idea of starting a lean journey came to the owners of Carel at the end of 2006. The founders, thanks to a well-established tradition of scientific collaboration with the University of Padua, learned the principles and techniques of Lean Thinking and initiated an internal discussion with management, calling into question the certainties resulting from years of growth and success. Francesco recalls, "At the end of 2006, Carel was preparing to close the year with sales and earnings in strong growth, but together with the owners and management, we realized that the group was beginning to lack a certain proactivity, the fervent drive to improve business processes while a sense of self-complacency and a lack of accountability was beginning to spread from the undeniable achievements of the group on a consolidated basis. Some 'happy islands' had formed, and there was fear that this sense of fulfilment could quickly spread throughout the company. In addition, some difficulties arose in communications between the different business areas, driven by an organizational structure that was functional, with delivery delays from the production department to the demands of the commercial department."

Furthermore, the development of new products had become an increasingly slow and complicated process, weighed down by the enormous variety of components used and the redundancies and confusion caused by the fact that in the functional organization project responsibility was shared by R&D and marketing, which worked sequentially. The focus of the development team ended up being fragmented by covering several projects simultaneously. A consequence of this situation was an average delay of 40% in the delivery of new product projects to production engineering that often sent back the proposals because they were too difficult, if not impossible, to implement according to the specifications, contributing to further lengthening the already unsatisfactory time to market.

The decision to introduce Lean Thinking initially was controversial even within the top management team. Francesco admits, "Although the chairman has always been attracted to Lean Thinking, I personally was a bit skeptical: My training and experiences fully reflected the definition of the modern manager given by Womack, namely, based on the traditional principles of functional organization and top-down authority with great confidence in the ability and heroism of individual managers rather than on the strength of the organization. But the owners kept pushing toward the lean approach, and I started to seriously gather information about it. When I began to understand the behavioral aspects and the application of the scientific method at the base of the Lean Thinking, I was immediately impressed and became its main operative sponsor."

An interesting aspect of Carel's lean journey, which is likely to have positively affected the outcome, is that Francesco was aware from the outset of the length and difficulty of undertaking a project of this magnitude. This awareness, far from discouraging the project, instead made him more determined to undertake it. In this regard, Francesco says, "In July 2007, a meeting was arranged between the owners and the management team, and at one point, the chairman stood up in front of everyone and officially announced to the managers that the company wanted to embark on a path of change according to the lean philosophy. This was the beginning of our formal process of change. The chairman, aware of the difficulties that would emerge but strongly determined to go all the way, said he wanted to establish a 'loyalty oath' with his employees. The owners were entirely willing to help those who encountered difficulties because of the change, while at the same time the managers were absolutely determined to carry forward the transformation process regardless of how many were potentially opposed to its realization."

Carel enlisted the help of a consulting firm (GMA and then JMAC), which proved decisive, especially in the early stages of the transformation. Having chosen an incremental approach to improvement and change, Francesco in September 2007 presented plans to the entire group to begin the lean transformation process. Nothing was left to chance: A program of meetings, seminars, internal workshops, and communication campaigns was started via the intranet and the corporate house organ in relation to the process that was being launched. A guide was drafted and distributed to all staff explaining the company's goals for the new year and the main pillars of Lean Thinking. In the following three months, they worked on the organizational review that resulted in the transition from a functional to a value stream organization with competence centers to which the transversal and multifunctional teams reported. Accepting this change was one of the hardest things; fear and resistance manifested at various levels also because the change implied revisions of job titles, changes in job descriptions, and changes in roles and positions within the organization. In particular, because the company was healthy from an economic and financial point of view and the need for change was not felt, it was necessary to create a strong sense of urgency showing all, sometimes even shockingly, the risks that the organization was running despite the success achieved up to that point. The creation of the sense of urgency certainly worked because at that time a rumor began circulating in the region where Carel is based that the company was on the brink of a precipice!

From an organizational point of view, a lean development office (LDO) was created with two full-time experts and a project manager. This office, which now has 10 lean experts at the group level, has the task of acquiring experience on lean methodologies to then be able to spread them in the organization and provide operational support to the multifunctional worksite, which has the role of implementing the change in practical terms.

A steering committee was also formed, a true leader of the transformation process, with planning and control functions, strategic orientation, and verification of the consistency between the business strategy and the lean process. This organ is composed of the board of directors, consultants, and key executives and currently meets bimonthly. Attending these meetings has been a truly unique experience for me and somewhat unique for Italian standards: strategically structured meetings and conversations in which the deployment of the corporate strategy is implemented through a portfolio of A3s aimed at resolving the main problems and facilitating the company's development.

Carel's lean journey has three significant aspects. The first is that it was somehow also the vehicle for the entrepreneurial and managerial succession process, which took place in a decisive but not a traumatic way—a truly rare event in medium-sized family businesses, in Italy as well as around the world. The second, exemplified by the extensive use of A3 also at the top level, is the adoption of Lean Thinking as a management system and not just a production system. The third is that the lean journey, instead of initiating on the shop floor as usually happens, started in the R&D department, that is, in the new product development process, which is the heart of a high technology–intensive company such as Carel.

The product development department has worked hard to break down the functional and physical walls. In fact, the office layout has been reorganized as an open space to increase cooperation, confrontation, and the rapid circulation of information. Today, borrowing the *obeya room* logic, the product development department is an open space with around 120 engineers that is characterized by the extensive use of visual management tools and totally inspired to lean product development principles.

Francesco is aware of the difficulties in sustaining the transformation and often monitors employee perceptions and satisfaction. He often uses this metaphor: "It's comparable to a marathon with many runners. The first are already halfway, but many are still at the starting gate. The top management and some leading people had had the opportunity and time to understand and digest the principles of the transformation, but most of the organization is still far behind."

One way to ensure alignment throughout the organization was the adoption of *hoshin kanri*, which allowed strategy deployment with strong involvement of all components of the organization. The company made these concepts its own with a program called Carel 2.0 with the stated goal of aligning the whole organization toward the key strategic objectives, its "true north." This continues today with the main long-term goals presented and discussed, identifying the areas of intervention. Each department is typically assigned an interdepartmental working group, called a "work stream" with a specific goal. In each work stream, different levels of the organization are represented but are always steered by a middle manager: Any top management involvement must be restricted to a supporting role. The work streams are in direct contact with the executive committee with whom they communicate in a modulated feedback process (catch ball) through A3s.

Lean Thinking was extended to the production department in 2009 with the start of the assembly to delivery (ATD) project. Thanks to production leveling and capacity control in final assembly, work orders are initiated depending on the actual shipment date. All this has enabled shortening customer waiting time and, at the same time, reducing the warehoused stock of finished products (speeding up transit).

The first production stages (prior to assembly) operate with a pull-type logic through the use of *kanban*: Upstream production and supply processes are activated based on actual consumption and the demands of downstream departments.

In the mechanical area, some U cells were created that operate on the principle of one-piece-flow within which each operator is responsible for the entire production cycle inasmuch as operators are polyvalent and their development is managed through appropriate skill maps. These mixed-model lines are replenished at regular intervals by dedicated logistics operators through specific material kits. In the electronics area, W cells were created (two attached U lines), in which the processes are stream-lined. This allowed eliminating a few levels in the bill of materials, greatly reducing the inventory and lead times. A water spider (power supply) is responsible for supplying the W lines at fixed intervals according to the pull system (a two-bin system).

The application of the single-minute exchange of die (SMED) technique to reduce setup times and the use of the largest possible number of stan-dardized components to be included in the products and then differenti-ated in the latter stages have led to a further shortening of material lead times.

The application of Lean Thinking has recently been extended to Chinese and American operations.

Francesco, in agreement with Chairman Luigi Rossi Luciani and CEO Luigi Nalini, certainly did not scrimp on resources on this path, and the investments in lean knowledge in the form of technology; changes in physical layout and processes; the establishment of a lean development office; acquiring external consultancy services; and the training of manag-ers, engineers, and operators were remarkable and continue to be because the sustainability of results requires relentless investments.

Periodically, "back to basics" programs are launched to further spread and sustain lean operation practices in all Carel plants. The program involves three basic tools: 5S, standardized work, and daily management.

What is the secret of success of lean transformation of Carel? Francesco has no doubts: "I think the commitment of top and middle management is crucial; the engineers, line workers, and salespeople must be able to see their leaders 'dirty' their hands on the *gemba* as workers do everyday, and the strong support of the owners is essential, which has never been absent in our company. In addition, to achieve true horizontal integration and better coordination between all the centers of competence, we need clear and direct communication within the group. But above all, the third necessary ingredient is the presence of lean agents, namely, competent technical personnel, experienced and passionate about Lean Thinking, energetic, caring, proactive bearers of lean values to promote them in the entire company. What's really hard to achieve is changes in the behavior of people in their daily habits and provide a glimpse of how change is cer-tainly an opportunity and not a risk."

1.6 THE BROVEDANI LEAN SYSTEM: BECOMING THE CHANGE WE WANT TO SEE

The first time I met the engineer Benito Zollia, chairman of the Brovedani Group, I was immediately struck by his manner and style: a gentleman of former times. I had heard of the Brovedani Group's lean transformation and knew the role as leader that Brovedani played in its region.

A man of few words but of great content, Benito Zollia is a passionate connoisseur of the history of science and technology, and this, combined with an unusual confidence in the ability of people to change and improve, is in some way a natural example of lean leadership. Goriziano, after a career in basketball at the highest national levels, in 1972 took over the workshop founded in 1947 by Silvio Brovedani. In 40 years, he transformed that workshop into a large industrial group. Today, Brovedani has 800 employees and six production units in Italy, Slovakia, and Mexico. The group is a world leader in business-to-business engineering (precision or "fine" as he likes to point out). In the last fifteen years, turnover increased from €53 million in 2001 to more than €100 million. The corporate headquarters, research, and engineering activities are located in San Vito al Tagliamento, in the province of Pordenone, in an area of Friuli Venezia Giulia that for almost half a century has been one of the great centers of the Italian engineering industry.

The application of Lean Thinking played a major role in ensuring the Brovedani Group's competitiveness and its ability to develop and internationalize in a difficult sector, such as precision mechanics, and in difficult years, such as those between 2009 and 2012.

This is how Sergio Barel, CEO of the group, remembers the start of the lean transformation: "In 2006, we saw that prices were falling all the time, costs went up, technical expertise was not enough; we had to find a new way of 'going back to the factory' to constantly improve processes. I attended a conference on Lean Thinking with some of my engineers. It was enlightening: We opened our minds, and we set off immediately. Again contrary to what is often the case, Brovedani did not start the application of Lean Thinking from factory production processes. The product development and industrialization process was essential for us to be able to remain competitive. We knew that we had to start from there. The technical department was turned inside out, and from there came a new organization of product development and industrialization, oriented by value stream and to the visibility of information. The results were not long in coming: For the same structure, around twice as many projects were managed and on-time production part approval process (PPAP) increased by 30%."

Sergio continues, "After the technical department, we assailed the factory, resulting in significant cost savings. The application of total productive maintenance (TPM) in all its pillars, area by area, allowed increasing the overall equipment effectiveness (OEE) by around 10 points, and reducing internal waste by 50%."

An emblematic episode of how the lean transformation process began concerns the setup time and the application of SMED techniques. "We operate in the field of precision engineering, and our customers are large international industrial companies, world leaders in their fields, who are highly demanding. Among others, we work for Delphi," says Sergio, and then remembers. "In 2007, a model change Delphi entailed 16 hours of downtime. Delphi's engineers regarded this as unacceptable and offered sending a lean expert to reduce this to 2 hours using SMED techniques; otherwise, we would lose the supply contract. Upon this, our engineers rebelled, a little out of pride, a little out of fear, and a little because it would mean, according to them, revealing our know-how to the customer. They came to me in droves to oppose it. I told them we could not lose this work. If we lost it, I would leave, but if we could reduce the setup time to 2 hours, I would commit myself to not sending anyone away. Indeed, if we accepted the challenge, we would learn how to do it! No sooner said than done. We worked with Delphi's engineers, and a few days later, the setup time was reduced to 2 hours. Not only did we not lose the work, but improved to the point that today we are Delphi's exclusive supplier, and the production area concerned has continued to improve even in the last year."

Also in the Brovedani case, activating the transformation process was not easy and required a great deal of energy and patience as well as appropriate methods and people. Sergio continues, "The main difficulties we encountered were not so much of a technical nature but of a relational and behavioral nature linked to people, their history with the company, their fear of change." During company visits and conversations with Sergio and his team of brilliant engineers, I was able to appreciate not only their in-depth knowledge of the principles and methods of Lean Thinking, but also their ability to reflect and learn from their experiences.

The resistance to change of those in charge of production was the main difficulty encountered in Brovedani. Faced with Lean Thinking concepts and methods, workers' and technicians' first reaction was 'it does not apply to us,' 'it cannot be done,' 'we are different,' 'our products are more complex,' 'we are already perfect,' 'we've always done it this way'... Sergio underlines, "The antidote to these difficulties, in some ways still present, was to resolve the problem according to the 'small steps' approach and pilot projects, creating the conditions so that every person could dedicate themselves to continuous improvement and innovation... We learned that only continuous, disciplined, and repeated exercising of the practices suggested by Lean Thinking could gradually destroy resistance to change and enabled creating a new mentality, greater responsibility, greater orientation toward the pursuit of perfection in the process."

Sergio Barel is a somewhat vivid example of the change achieved in Brovedani. A mechanical engineer with design experience in the oil platform industry, he has worked at Brovedani for more than 20 years. During these years, he led the development of the company along the lines foreseen by the chairman and using the application of Lean Thinking to complete Brovedani's managerial transition. Even in this case, as in others recounted in this chapter, the skill and energy of the Brovedani management team, and particularly the quality of young people responsible for the technical and production departments, is striking.

"Engage! Engage! Engage!" Sergio always repeats, "We know that an imposed decision is more difficult to accept and implement than a joint decision. Lack of involvement, lack of understanding of the reasons, lack of information and skills generate discomfort, an incorrect interpretation of what is being done as well as a certain distrust and a sense of exclusion that leads people to activate defensive and uncooperative behaviors... Another aspect that we have given particular importance to with the application of Lean Thinking is evidencing and sharing the results. The nonsharing of results typically generates a sense of futility of the efforts and commitment made, along with the belief that 'in any case, nothing will ever change...' Putting significant results and the people who achieved them under the spotlight has enabled obtaining a dual result: spreading knowledge across the organization and motivating/rewarding the players for their achievements."

Sergio and his management team know that the Brovedani lean system must always be nurtured in order to remain useful and that paradoxically it could itself become an obstacle to continuous improvement. He offered me this metaphor, "The application of Lean Thinking is like an antibiotic: On one hand, its strength is in constant use because change is a process of collective learning and learning is not attained in leaps; it is progressive.

On the other, it has to be used appropriately, in such a way as to maintain the tension constantly toward continuous improvement and avoid the risk of habituation. Lean Thinking can itself become routine. Focusing on tools and practices, no longer looking for improvement and becoming convinced of having arrived with nothing more to be achieved. Lean transformation is instead an ongoing process that should be continuously pursued and revitalized with precise techniques."

One of the elements that characterizes the successful application of Lean Thinking in Brovedani is the organizational aspect. There is strong synergy, integration, and coordination among the activities of the lean promotion office and the human resources and production functions, and this has allowed activating the process of restructuring the organization of the production structure. Brovedani's plants were structured according to the microplant logic (organizational units ascribable to the value stream concept). This has led to a redefinition of the roles and responsibilities (particularly middle management), the direct/indirect relationships (and span of support), and the mapping of the expertise of team members, which has allowed understanding the differences between current and expected levels by type of expertise and hence the related training gaps.

In sum, through the application of the Lean Thinking principles and techniques, the Brovedani Group was able to remain a leader in the application of the most advanced methods in the production of precision engineering components, ensuring the highest standards of quality in small- and large-volume production. The Brovedani lean system supports the group's development strategy through international plants, which enable serving customers better with just-in-time supplies and to work in very close partnerships in the spirit of full service leadership. The strengths of the Brovedani Group are its organization and creativity as witnessed by the abundant innovative content brought into the field of B2B fine engineering in product design as well as in the parallel and cross-functional production processes and their industrialization. This innovative spirit has contributed to the success of the Brovedani Group, which is now a strategic supplier of multinational companies, such as Bosch, Continental, Daimler, Delphi, Eaton, Magna, Magneti Marelli, Sanden, VCS, and others.

In short, Brovedani is today a worldwide leader in providing technological solutions, wherever precision engineering is a critical success factor—a company rooted in its history and proud of its values, made up of people who are able to grow and aggregate, open to different cultures and experiences to conquer the future and a company that has Lean Thinking as its foundational philosophy that inspires and directs the group's growth day after day.

1.7 TRANSFORMING SMALL AND MEDIUM ENTERPRISES

The stories of Mario Nardi, Ezio Bruno, Enrico Franzolin, Francesco Nalini, and Sergio Barel are stories of small and medium enterprises (SMEs) that contain, in a series of corporate microcosms, all the issues and challenges of doing business in industry in Italy as elsewhere. They show how Lean Thinking represents an extraordinary opportunity for SMEs to change, develop, grow, and innovate. Pietro Fiorentini, Frandent, Unox, Carel, and Brovedani are all examples of lean transformations, that is, of companies moving from an old way of thinking to Lean Thinking. As illustrated by all the cases, such change requires a complete transformation on how a company conducts business, takes a long-term perspective and perseverance, is based on value streams metrics that eventually drive every line item in a financial statement in the right direction, and entails the building of a lean culture (Koenigsaecker, 2009).

A successful lean transformation seldom happens by chance. It takes a lot of work, wise use of resources, a thorough knowledge of Lean Thinking, organizational change skills, and patience.

The cases illustrated in this chapter show that, SMEs' owners, entrepreneurs, and managers have to commit to do the following (Byrne, 2012):

1. Undertake a personal "lean journey."
2. Learn the four fundamental principles of Lean Thinking: work at *takt time*, create one-piece flow, establish standard work, and connect your customer to your shop floor through a pull system.
3. Articulate a strategy, set stretch goals, define the core values to lead the team, and obtain expert lean knowledge to train everyone up front.
4. Change the organizational structure, possibly moving toward value stream–based units, and create trust and commitment by making sure that no layoffs will result from *kaizen* initiatives.

5. Lead the transformation yourself, in the *gemba*, participating in all improvement activities and relentlessly communicating and motivating the whys and hows of the transformation.
6. Lead the transformation always from the front in a hands-on way, taking leaps of faith when necessary and acknowledging successes and failures.
7. Change the way you monitor performance and related systems.
8. Capitalize the gains coming from the transformation, reinvesting them in the business and sharing them with employees and partners.

In the next chapters, after providing some background about the context in which the transformations narrated in this chapter took place, we will offer a framework to interpret lean transformations in SMEs, a set of typical lean transformation patterns, as well as their antecedents, triggering, and facilitating factors. We will also offer evidence, based on large-scale original research, about the typical financial dynamics of SMEs' lean transformations, providing guidelines about what to expect during the transformation process, how to design it, and what potential mistakes to avoid.

Italy, known for its industrial system prevalently based on SMEs and often studied as a benchmark for other countries in this regard, will provide the empirical ground from which to learn lessons that can be generalized across industries, regions, and countries.

2

Understanding the Italian Context

2.1 *SENSEI* LUCIANO

I met Luciano Massone in the early '90s at the meetings of the International Motor Vehicle Program at MIT, and we have kept in touch ever since, almost like two "distance travellers" in the Italian lean movement.

I consider Luciano one of the few Italian *sensei* (masters). He has achieved this role through three decades of hard work in the Fiat Group, a company in which he has held a variety of key roles: from project leader to director of human resources at the Melfi plant (the first Fiat plant—a greenfield plant—designed according to the principles of the Toyota Production System), from chief industrial relations officer to his current role as vice president of EMEA World Class Manufacturing, a position that engages him on both sides of the Atlantic as he is also senior auditor for the Chrysler plants.

The development and widespread adoption of world class manufacturing (WCM)—the production system* the Fiat-Chrysler group adopts in all its plants worldwide and which also incorporates the lessons learned by Fiat from Toyota—has undoubtedly been one of the highlights and secrets of the industrial revival of the Marchionne Fiat era. The new impetus to the adoption of WCM began in 2005, the year after the arrival of Marchionne, when an organizational unit focused on the implementation of WCM was formed at the central level.

Luciano, with his then small team of engineers (at the time only 4 and now nearly 500 specialists scattered around the world) experimented with the WCM techniques, initially creating two model plants at Melfi and Tychy (Poland). The performance improvements in these two pilot plants

---

* WCM is a formalized system of tools, practices, and behavioral routines that largely draws from the Toyota production system (Schonberger, 1986; Yamashina, 1995, 1996; Yamashina and Kubo, 2002). It revolves around five pillars: safety (eliminate all types of accidents), quality (eliminate defects), productivity (eliminate waste), technical efficiency (eliminate breakdowns), and service (just-in-time).

were impressive. Since the implementation of WCM in the Tychy plant, the number of improvement proposals in seven months per employee increased 7.5-fold from 0.45 to 3.5 with an adoption rate of 50%. At Melfi, defects of electrical controls on the Grande Punto (Fiat's top selling model in Europe at the time) were reduced by 50% in nine months.

Stefan Ketter became responsible for manufacturing, and Luciano then formalized the system and extended it to all the Fiat Group Automobiles plants and later also to the other companies of the group (from IVECO to CNH, from Magneti Marelli to Chrysler).

Today, WCM is *the* Fiat Group's production system, and the results that Luciano has helped to achieve are truly remarkable: The number of development/improvement initiatives increased from 2400 in 2006 to 21,600 in 2009 and 39,000 in 2010 with more than 1 million improvement proposals made each year; from 2006 to 2009, the Italian and Polish car plants' productivity increased by 20% and 25%, respectively, as defects, rework, breakdowns, and activities deemed non–added value, such as changes resulting from nonoptimal layouts or timing were reduced. In the same period, absenteeism was also reduced by 14% at the group level, and workplace safety improved significantly with a significant reduction in the frequency and severity rates of accidents (in 2010–2015 the frequency and severity rates went further down by 73% and 69%, respectively).

Estimates at the group level at the beginning of the transformation envisaged an aggregate cost savings of 500 million euros to be achieved in five years, thus by the end of 2010. At the end of 2009, the estimates had already been far exceeded with actual savings that amounted to 730 million euros. In early 2010, the estimates foresaw that for that year and for future years up to 2014 cumulative savings would reach 1.9 billion euros but were later significantly revised. For the 2011–2014 period, the new estimates indicated average savings of 6% per annum compared with the operating costs of the previous period for a total value of 2.6 billion euros. On top of this, during a decade, WCM has been applied in more than 200 plants around the globe, training 500 specialists, executing 65,000 projects and generating nearly 10 million suggestions.

These results, which must be added to those obtained in the ex-Chrysler plants, are truly remarkable, but even more remarkable is the personal story of Luciano Massone, who in 2004 had the courage to change his professional career, to invest in himself by moving to Japan for a "sabbatical" year, to question himself by abandoning the certainties deriving from more than a decade of experience and professional achievements to become a *deshi* (disciple), choosing a master such as Hajime Yamashina and truly learning by "doing," immersing himself in details, and gaining knowledge of the principles and techniques that can only come from their continuous exercising and profound understanding.

The story of Luciano Massone—like those of Mario Nardi and the companies, managers, and entrepreneurs described in Chapter 1—suggests that it is not possible to transform businesses without first transforming themselves, and to do so requires defining the personal routines to remain in the learning mode, to develop their own *kata* (Rother, 2009) or those behavioral habits that enable open-mindedness, be they (as in the case of Luciano Massone) the ferocious factory audits of Prof. Yamashina or practicing the sport of sailing at a high level.

Every so often I call him, and Luciano always answers with patience and kindness, despite his myriad duties and responsibilities on both sides of the ocean. When I go to see him in Turin, he shows me the new initiatives and tells me about increasingly ambitious challenges, from the A3 portfolio, the patenting of technical solutions resulting from the continuous improvement activities, to the application of WCM to suppliers. In the safe in his office, he keeps the diplomas and certificates awarded him and, if asked, shows them with great pride.

Also in this case, we are not looking at changes obtained through flamboyant leadership that forces results but the ability to listen and understand, the determination to identify problems and patience in understanding their root cause and finding the solutions, together with others, without presumptions, through engagement and discussion in accordance with the scientific method and doing so also and especially in terms of the ever-difficult internal or external context of the Fiat Chrysler Automobile Group.

I chose to start this chapter on the evolution of the lean movement in Italy mentioning Luciano Massone because over the course of almost 30 years with Fiat he has witnessed this development in its different phases as well as the difficulties and resistance to managerial innovation that Lean Thinking entails—in Italy as elsewhere—and not only due to union opposition.

2.2 LEAN THINKING AND ITALY

At the end of the '70s, the penetration of the Japanese automakers in Western markets surprised European and American manufacturers.

According to the scholars of the time, the success of the Japanese was mainly due to their country system with its specific cultural and institutional as well as exogenous determinants related to international trade regulations. Only after a period of partial denial and rejection did they realize that the success of Japanese producers was attributable to the production system they adopted and that it was also adoptable by European and North American manufacturers as demonstrated by the more than positive results obtained by Japanese companies in their American and European transplants (Womack, Jones, and Roos, 1990; Kenney and Florida, 1991; Garrahan and Stewart, 1992).

The dissemination of the Lean Thinking principles and techniques occured later in Italian companies, initially affecting only a handful of large firms. Only in the last decade Lean Thinking has been applied extensively also in SMEs.

If, as mentioned earlier, the socioeconomic characteristics of Japan contributed to the success of the Toyota system, then it is possible that the particularities of the Italian industrial system historically influenced and continue to influence the way Lean Thinking was introduced in Italy.

The key particularities of the Italian context include the small size of the businesses, flexibility, creativity, and spirit of improvisation that characterize production and business activities; family ownership and the widespread involvement of family members in business management; firms belonging to local clusters/territorial districts with strong interorganizational connections. Given these characteristics and taking into account the exemplar experiences reported in Chapter 1, it is interesting to analyze how Italian companies and, more importantly, the people who work in them, adopt and adapt the principles and tools of Lean Thinking.

2.2.1 Focusing on SMEs

Everyone agrees that SMEs are the most dynamic and proactive part of the any economy, and these are the entities on which to focus for the development that in time will prove virtuous and sustainable for Italy and many other countries. The great recession started in 2008 somewhat forced companies to engage in a lean transformation. In some cases, we witnessed "desperate" lean programs with lean seen as the last resort as firms became permanently crippled by the crisis either financially or in terms of the compatibility of their cost structure. In other cases, lean programs were initiated primarily to reduce cost and recover margins that were gradually eroding from ever-increasing competitive pressure. In some other cases instead, more alert SMEs' owners, entrepreneurs, and managers grasped the innovative, holistic, and cultural nature lean transformation processes and seized the opportunity to drastically change through applying Lean Thinking. As the cases illustrated in Chapter 1 show, lean transformations allowed the successful modification of business models and corporate mentality, effectively dealing with significant changes, organizational resistance, and conflict (with the trade unions, with management, and with other family members in the case of family businesses). The leaders of these firms not only focused on the technical and production aspects, but attempted to involve all organizational actors—employees, suppliers, and customers, investing heavily in Lean Thinking tools to change their mentality. This in the belief that, faced with the progress of emerging countries and the impossibility and injustice to reducing local labor costs, the management system subtending Lean Thinking could be a formidable weapon to regain efficiency and competitiveness.

However, the diffusion of Lean Thinking in Italy cannot be separated from the abovementioned particularities that are in part enabling factors of the adoption of Lean Thinking and in part potential obstacles and difficulties.

Local clusters/territorial districts where companies are highly interconnected geographically as well as culturally are an enabling factor in the adoption of interorganizational collaborations and the extended enterprise approach Lean Thinking postulates (Jones and Womack, 2011). For example, thanks to geographical proximity and through adopting pull logic, customers can easily pull production from the supplier, collaborate in solving problems, optimize the supply chain (not the individual production function), and jointly design a single value stream that goes from the upstream supplier to the end customer. Coordination intended in these terms allows reducing the variability and related inefficiencies linked to the bullwhip effect,* reducing inventories (sometimes duplicated in the supplier's end product warehousing and in the customer's material warehousing) and the resulting costs, optimizing logistics flows (customer-supplier synchronous *kanban*, lower transportation costs, etc.),

---

* This consists of enlarging the variability of the behavior of a complex system managed sequentially and is based on the principles of industrial dynamics originally theorized by Forrester (1964) and subsequently consolidated by the theory of system dynamics developed by Senge (1990) and Sterman (2000). Due to delays and problems in the feedback circuits of physical and information flows, in a complex system managed separately and sequentially (e.g., supply chain), greater variability and inefficiencies occur if the single elements are individually optimized.

and reducing the impact of variability on organic production and employment. On the other hand, operating in the lean supply chain perspective leads to increased organizational complexity (and contractual relationships) and greater logistical fragility, necessary for the development of just-in-time supply, as well as a potential negative effect in terms of local transport network congestion and air pollution.

A further factor enabling the application of Lean Thinking in Italian SMEs is the possibility of implementing changes and organizational improvements in less time. Small size renders the lean transformation processes potentially more effective and rapid. As the stories in the first chapter illustrate, with strong commitment and appropriate skills and leadership, the processes and their physical and information flows can be redesigned more easily through direct contact with customers, people can be involved more directly and easily, and the results of improvement activities become visible in less time. On the other hand, small size is generally synonymous with low managerial levels, destructuring, and indiscipline. Small businesses are often undercapitalized (that is, they significantly rely on debt). Resources are often unavailable for dedicated investments, or if available, they are not sufficient to reach the minimum scale. For example, when small businesses consider undertaking a lean transformation, it becomes difficult to hire and develop Lean Thinking capabilities, be they in the form of competent people, training and consulting services, or internal *sensei* able to drive the transformation. The alternative route, as illustrated by some of the cases reported in Chapter 1, is SME owners, entrepreneurs, and/or managers taking it upon themselves to learn and change firsthand and then begin the transformation. In such cases, the outcomes differ depending on how profound and genuine the entrepreneur's personal transformation has been, both in terms of learning the Lean Thinking principles and techniques and the change in mentality. Given the degree of decision-making centralization and operational involvement in management, in small business only "thoroughly transformed" entrepreneurs are typically able to engender effective business transformations. Precisely here, the other particularity of the Italian system emerges, that is, the diffusion of family ownership and the operational involvement of the family in business management. Applying the Lean Thinking principles and techniques is facilitated if all family members involved in management share the same approach and are familiar with the techniques and dynamics. The application itself can be used as a discontinuity to manage entrepreneurial and managerial succession. Adhering to the principles of Lean Thinking and the ability of mastering the techniques could even become the criterion for selecting entrepreneurial and managerial resources. On the other hand, a lean transformation can become a source of great internal conflict among family members and even inhibit the entrepreneurial succession process, especially when the Lean Thinking principles and techniques are exploited for purposes of power or are applied mimetically without substantially contaminating the management system and decision-making approach.

Overall, our research suggests that the aspects that differentiate lean-transformed Italian SMEs from the others are the following: (a) the application of the scientific method as a pillar of the decision-making process and (b) the collegiality of decision making. The first aspect is particularly important because, on one hand, operational propensity is innate in SMEs' owners and managers—in Italy as elsewhere—as well as to stay closely in contact with production and trade realities, which is one of the fundamental characteristics of lean leadership (the principle of *genchi genbutsu* or "seeing firsthand" to understand the situation and the problems); on the other hand, there is a noted general reluctance to structure and systematize such observation; to critically reflect on their own style and management system; and to collect in a rigorous, structured, and repeatable way data and information that may corroborate or falsify the hypothesized plans or decisions. This element of managerial discipline, referred to in the literature as evidence-based management (Pfeffer and Sutton, 2000, 2006), results in the application of rigorous problem-solving methods at all levels. But it is lacking in many SMEs. More eclectic and intuitive approaches are often preferred by owners, entrepreneurs, and managers that involve less robust decisions and produce more volatile results. The second aspect is complementary to the first in the sense that a management system such as that based on Lean Thinking and on operational evidence and the continuous improvement approach cannot but use *all* the energy, skills, and knowledge available within a given SME. This assumes that only decision-making processes that involve everyone (from the strategy deployment perspective) enable incorporating the entire body of corporate knowledge and empower people to identify problems and take actions to solve them. Many Italian SMEs—but my sense is that this applies also elsewhere—are led one-directionally, with decision-making processes that are focused and fast but not verified or shared. Such a management system, dominated by the "splendid solitude" of the SME's owner, entrepreneur, or a few key players in the firm, is more fragile when the complexity of issues increases, and the risks associated with the decisions (and possible errors) are higher.

The characteristics of the Italian industrial system and the nature of the prevailing production specialization of Italian SMEs leads to further considerations in terms of why and how to undertake a lean transformation. Italian SMEs are often in direct competition with international manufacturers from emerging economies that enjoy lower labor costs. The adoption of the Lean Thinking principles and techniques has by now become almost mandatory to regain competitiveness with respect to these competitors but also to develop the capability to remain competitive, changing, and improving continuously (Fujimoto, 1999; Kogut and Kulatilaka, 2001; Anand et al., 2009). In this sense, for an SME, a lean transformation means not only and not so much a punctual solution to regaining competitiveness and productivity today, but a dynamic solution to ensure remaining competitive tomorrow, regardless of the specific challenges that companies face.

In other words, having an organization that enables applying techniques such as 5S, VSM, A3, voice of the customer, standardized work, one-piece-flow, TPM, SMED, *kanban*, *hoshin kanri*, and so forth could be the most effective solution to repositioning the business and recovering profitability in the short term, but it is also a set of management routines (the management system, in fact) that can be used tomorrow to continue improving.

Undertaking a lean transformation requires, from the SME owners, entrepreneurs, and managers, a reinterpretation of the concept of organization, management, and operational work. A clear example of this in Italian SMEs is the perception of the concept of work standardization, very different from the Italian sensibility, which instead constitutes a fundamental element of any lean transformation. Standardized work (studying and sharing the best way of doing things that everyone applies until a better way is proven and to continue experimenting in this sense) applies to operators and management. It consists of rules that guide actions and form the basis of any improvement. This is the opposite with respect to the individual and unrepeatable approach that sometimes (and inappropriately) is an integral part of the DNA of SMEs, their entrepreneurs–artists/heroes and their workers–artisans.

In Italy, decades of poor applications of Fordism and labor unrest, obvious or latent, legitimate or ideological, have resulted in losing sight of the question of work and the need to improve the content and methods according to the canons of science and equity. As we will see in Chapter 3, standardized work is the tool for this, to be applied in conjunction with others and particularly with the support of techniques of continuous training such the training within industry (TWI) programs (Dinero, 2005). The widespread application of standardized work, defined not based on abstract and general metrics, such as MTM or Ergo-UAS, or by work measurement specialists, but according to the actual experience of workers and through a shared process, undoubtedly improves work productivity as well as the safety and ergonomics of many Italian SMEs. There is a great need for practical experimentation and not abstract and instrumental discussions to acquire positions of power in labor relations.

On the other hand, the application of standardized work in many SMEs cannot but differ from that which occurs in Toyota or even in Fiat-Chrysler assembly plants. It is one thing to apply standardized work when the plant's *takt time* is around 60 seconds and another when it is instead applied to fashion apparel work at Corneliani, where the cycle time is much longer, work content is much more variable and professionalism of workers is much more complex, or at Ducati, where the workers are so highly trained and qualified (as well as passionate about motorbikes) that they know how to assemble and disassemble the whole bike themselves. The challenge for Italian SMEs is how to impart the discipline needed to achieve efficiency and continuous generalized improvements inherent in standardized work and teamwork in an industrial culture that is very oriented toward production understood as ad hoc solutions to problems considered unique and unrepeatable to individualism, unstructured creativity, inspiration.

Finally, one last consideration on the role of trade unions that, as everybody knows, play an important role in Italy as well as in other countries. Lean Thinking promotes the active participation and involvement of all employees; it thus seems obvious that if convinced of its revolutionary significance in terms of involvement, empowerment, and the contribution of all, the task of the unions should be to promote and facilitate any SME undertaking a lean transformation and at best to work in partnership with the owners and managers in its design and execution. However, the context of industrial relations—in Italy as well as elsewhere—might be characterized by rigidity, mistrust, and difficulties at every level. Such an environmental factor runs the risk of distorting a lean transformation and eventually may lead it to failure because of two dangerous ideologies (Accornero, 2009). The first—on the employers' side—is that of "smuggling," through a lean transformation, simple practices of work intensification and job insecurity associated with systematic workforce downsizing. The second—on the unions' side—is demanding employment guarantees, organizational democratization, and human capital investments without linking these to the principles of accountability and the flexible use of human resources.

2.2.2 The Wisdom of Eng. Alberto

In 1989, while at MIT as a graduate student, I complemented my scholarship reviewing books for the Italian business magazine *Mondo Economico*. The magazine used to send me some of the most interesting Italian books on management, paid me to review them (I will leave the amount to the reader's imagination), and allowed me to keep the books. One day I received the book *La Qualità Totale* [*Total Quality*] by Alberto Galgano (1990). I devoured the book and fell in love with the themes of total quality management and company wide quality control. So it was that on returning to Italy and having sent him the review, I met Eng. Alberto Galgano, certainly a pioneer and one of the greatest protagonists of the Italian lean movement.

Alberto Galgano is now recognized by all as a wise sage of the Italian lean movement and with his history and personality, in my opinion, well represents the principles and concepts of Lean Thinking.

I believe four fundamental characteristics have marked his professional career that began in the '50s. The first is the conviction—if you like an almost outmoded positivism—that management, as a practice and theory, should also be scientifically based. The belief in the scientific method, which perhaps also stems from the fact that Eng. Galgano graduated in chemical engineering at the Politecnico di Milano with Professor Giulio Natta, Nobel Prize in Chemistry, is associated with the second characteristic, namely, rigor in analyzing problems, which is expressed in both the philosophy of a diagnostic business approach and in his often critical writings on the evils of Italian industry and the possible remedies. The recurrence is striking with which his books, in particular *Toyota. Perchè l'industria italiana non progredisce* [*Toyota. Why Italian Industry Does Not Progress*] (Galgano, 2005), are cited as the inspiration for the start of lean transformations in many Italian SMEs.

The third characteristic is—if you will—a corollary of the second, namely, the intransigence and rigor required of SMEs' owners, entrepreneurs, managers, and workers and the corresponding determination and absence of compromise for anyone who wishes to engage in a lean transformation. This characteristic is very similar to what I find distinguishes Toyota's management, especially in Japan and among the direct and indirect students of Taiichi Ohno in the operations management consulting division of Toyota—finally, the constant reminder of Italian humanistic and scientific (especially Renaissance) tradition and the need to refer back to it to grow and prosper.

Eng. Galgano is a privileged witness of the vices and virtues of the Italian SMEs and his professional career, characterized by belief in the scientific method, rigor, and intransigence and also recalling the Italian tradition, constitutes the testing ground for Italian companies that want Lean Thinking to be the starting point of innovating their management systems.

2.3 A SHORT HISTORY OF THE ITALIAN LEAN MOVEMENT

Based on these premises, the historical evolution of the lean movement in Italy can be interpreted along two axes: the first, which corresponds to some historical macrophases, and the second, which corresponds instead to some dissemination paths of Lean Thinking, paths that have intertwined and disentangled in managerial practice and academic research, according to different application contexts, the actors involved, and their underlying approach. These paths have diversified, intersected, and recombined in the evolution of the Italian lean movement despite starting from the common matrix of the study and interpretation of the Toyota production system.

2.3.1 From Total Quality Management to Lean Thinking

Many of the Lean Thinking principles and techniques have their natural historical antecedents in total quality management (TQM; Juran and De Feo, 2010), which then became one of the operational tools of Lean Thinking. TQM emphasizes quality in processes and products through the involvement of all individuals who make up the organization, from the top management to workers. The origins of TQM date back to Shewhart's pioneering studies on statistical process control and those carried out in the '50s when the Japanese Union of Scientists and Engineers (JUSE) hosted the lessons of Deming on statistical process control. In 1954, Juran with the *Quality Control Handbook* shifted focus onto the managerial aspects of quality, holding courses on quality management for top and middle managers. The quality revolution involved the entire company: Quality control had to be first and foremost the responsibility of the management and not just a corporate function in charge of quality. In subsequent years, some Japanese experts, including Prof. Ishikawa, elaborated on the contributions in the field of total quality, including those of Deming and Juran, and systematized them into the Company Wide Quality Control model whose principles were formalized in 1968. The innovative concept deriving from this new approach was the introduction of customer satisfaction: quality meant not only meeting the standards of product quality and reliability but also compliance with customer needs.

The concept of total quality, which spread to Japan in the '50s, arrived in the West only in the late '70s, when European and American companies became aware of the growing gap between their products and those of the Japanese, and thus the "discovery of quality in the Western world" (Galgano, 1990).

However, companies proved unprepared to accept and integrate the new method for cultural reasons (for TQM to function, the overall organizational mindset had to change) and for technical reasons (lacking the knowledge and means with which to measure and manage quality). Beyond these gaps, which in time were overcome, the failures of the first total quality projects in Italy are to be ascribed to a lack of universal understanding. In fact, the first implementations were mere imitation of one or more of the most famous aspects of company wide quality control (and in particular quality circles) but without capitalizing on their comprehensive cultural and organizational implications.

In Italy, the first steps toward the implementation of the Lean Thinking principles and techniques took place in the '80s. In the first half of that decade, Italian companies had experienced the phenomenon of quality circles, but in many cases, the results of their application were compromised by the belief that the adoption of this tool could lead to rapid improvements leaving the organizational structure unchanged.

The application of TQM and lean production began to spread and became known in the Italian corporate world only when Cesare Romiti, then the CEO of Fiat, in 1989 gave the green light to total quality at Fiat. In a famous speech at the FIAT management meeting in Marentino, Cesare Romiti declared that the Japanese competition, based on the concept of total quality and *kaizen*, was threatening the very survival of Western automotive manufacturers, highlighting the urgent need to adapt production methods and approaches to remain competitive (Merli, 1991). At the end of the '80s, the market difficulties related to strong competition from automobile manufacturers around the world, and particularly those in Japan, exposed the strategic and organizational weaknesses of Fiat. These factors triggered a profound restructuring process.

2.3.2 The First Phase of Development: Quality Circles

Quality circles were an emblematic element of the Japanese model. Ishikawa defined the circles as "a small group of people (8–10) in the same work area and with similar tasks, who meet regularly and voluntarily under the guidance of a coordinator, learning to identify and analyze the problems of their work, to propose solutions, implement them, test them, and measure the effects."

In Italy, quality circles were introduced on an experimental basis in 1972 at SNIA Viscosa and in 1978 at Ire Ignis. From 1980 to 1981, the phenomenon slowly began to spread in companies of all sizes, in the most diverse sectors, from manufacturing to service companies (Gualtieri, 1985). However, these procedures were introduced as an isolated tool within a traditional mass production schema without triggering the organizational change deemed necessary by the Japanese model. According to those who described the phenomenon, the diffusion of circles after an initial "fashionable" period garnered greater awareness of the usefulness of the principles adopted in the mid-'80s, and then a decline began that coincided with the conceptual study of total quality in academia and business (Merli, 1985).

The initial phase immediately exposed some problems mainly related to two reasons:

- Insufficient knowledge of the model and insufficient support from management, convinced that quality circles related only to operational staff
- Inadequate training of operators in terms of problem solving

Because management involvement, adequate corporate reorganization, and a precise training path are prerequisites for the effective functioning of the circles, it is fairly easy to understand why some of these experiences failed. In these cases, the reason that often led to adopting the circles was instead the desire to achieve short-term goals or simply wanting to boast about using a "fashionable" management tool.

In 1985, Galgano Consulting surveyed the adoption of quality circles in Italian companies. From his research emerged that around 90 companies among the first Italian industrial companies had already begun quality circles, and a further 90 would start them soon. Among the companies surveyed, about 400 circles were operating, but the percentage of employees involved was rather low: less than 2%. The research also brought to light that the underlying reasons for their adoption were technical–operational and socio-motivational. Although the results of this survey demonstrated the lively interest of Italian companies in the quality circles programs, the phenomenon basically turned out to be a managerial fashion with rare and modest results in the short term. This was in contrast to the need of many companies to achieve a cultural change requiring efforts that would not peter out in a few years.

In an interview in 1985, the CEO of SNIA Fibre—a company that in those years was a pioneer of quality—suggested that those preparing to take the same path he had taken should "Find the courage to consider quality as a priority issue, dedicate a great deal of time to it, identify managers who have the same beliefs, and then proceed without hesitation, be willing in spite of some initial unsuccessful attempts."

This recommendation remained largely unheeded at least for a few years.

2.3.3 The Second Phase of Development: The Fiat Case

Quality circles were therefore the means with which the first quality and continuous improvement approaches were introduced by Italian firms in the early '80s. Moreover, at that time, the introduction of such an approach was limited to the technical–production functions and usually entrusted to specifically charged quality management. However, after 1988, the conceptual framework was gradually expanded and extended beyond industrial processes and also oriented toward the market and commercial activities. The reconceptualization of the process was accompanied by a new interest in putting the voice of the customer at the center, and the idea established that it would somehow be conveyed within many, if not all organizational processes. At least in intention, customers and their satisfaction were identified as the fundamental business objectives to be pursued through the quality of the product or service that the customer bought. The approach thus rethought would involve the entire value chain from the supplier to the end customer.

The most significant example of this shift to the philosophy of quality and subsequently to the Toyota production system was Fiat and particularly the attempt to implement the principles of Lean Thinking through the *Fabbrica Integrata* ("integrated factory") model (Bonazzi, 1993).

In the '80s, Fiat was still fully anchored to the principles of mass production, in some ways particularly due to the high degree of vertical integration, a strong presence in the domestic market (in which it held an almost monopolistic market share of 60%), and production mainly focused on a difficult-to-penetrate foreign market segment (utilitarian cars). Moreover, the last two aspects affected the company's margins, which depended heavily on the performance of the domestic market. The combination and the escalation of these circumstances, the launch of cars on the market by foreign producers in direct competition and the cost gap with other manufacturers (especially the Japanese) led the Turin-based company to launch a reorganization plan at the end of the '80s that involved all the activities and actors (including suppliers and distributors) contributing to the production and marketing of vehicles.

At Fiat's management convention in Marentino that took place in October 1989, Fiat's CEO Cesare Romiti asked the engineer Giorgio Merli—consultant to the Galgano Group and an expert on Japanese industry—to illustrate the potential of just-in-time to eliminate the unproductive factors and exalt production flexibility. However, importing the Toyota model to Italy required revolutionizing the way people thought and worked, it required involving people and reviewing the organizational hierarchical and functional model of the management approach based on command and control. The plan presented on this occasion foresaw five years of work structured in interventions on three levels: the company as a whole, the functional areas, and the microprocesses and individual activities.

In 1991, with Paolo Cantarella appointed CEO of the Turin-based company, the five-year plan was divided into 20 macrospecific initiatives for change and improvement. In support of this reorganization, an investment of 40,000 billion lire was planned up to the year 2000 with which to launch 20 new car models, two per year. This would be possible by reducing the time to market thanks to the adoption of methods such as simultaneous engineering (performing engineering and design tasks in parallel), codesigning with suppliers, and carrying over the development activities of the new product. The changes involved the entire production chain and in particular the plants, reorganized according to the principles of Lean Thinking along the lines implemented in the greenfield plant in Melfi as well as the actors involved upstream (suppliers) and downstream (distribution) (Volpato, 2004).

Fiat thus began its reorganization by reviewing relationships with suppliers (Camuffo and Volpato, 1997c). They wanted to recognize their strategic role in contributing to the quality and cost of a car and thus the need for a coordination and collaboration program. One of the main objectives was to implement just-in-time supply. The location of suppliers in adjacent lots to the assembly lines (at the Melfi factory around 700,000 m² were allocated to suppliers) was intended to significantly reduce supply lead times. This new supply chain approach marked, at least in intention, a sharp reversal of the trend toward vertical integration and the adversarial supply relationships that had always characterized Fiat. In the face of such revolutionary changes, internal resistors abounded who were tied to a vision of Fiat that had hitherto based their supply relationships on tenders and short-term contracts. However, with the new program, the Turin-based company had initiated more cooperative relationship policies with suppliers based on trust, on long-term contracts, on comakership, policies that resulted in reducing the number of suppliers and the degree of vertical integration.

This was accompanied, at least for some components and some plants, by the introduction of a supply-pull logic based on supermarkets and *kanban* and, in some cases, on supply-flow in synchronous *kanban*.

Similar intentions and initiatives were also launched for the sales network and after-sales services (Buzzavo, 2008). This was a highly strategic area as generally dealers interfaced with end customers. In observance, at least in the abstract, of the lean principle of focusing on the customer, a Fiat car would not only respond to the requirements of convenience, to a very good quality/price ratio, but also to a better and more effective after-sales service that would provide customer care. Given these assumptions, the commercial strategy was aimed at improving customer satisfaction (the Customer Satisfaction Index or CSI was introduced), building customer loyalty and conceiving and implementing new procedures for a closer partnerships with dealers (the rationalization and development of which began by also innovating the information system with the Sirio and Focus initiatives).

The focal point of the first Fiat reorganization according to the dictates of Lean Thinking was the transition from a high automation factory to an integrated factory (IF) in the assembly plants (Camuffo and Micelli, 1999). According to the IF formula, the integration of processes and governance of organizational interdependencies were the drivers of productivity. The key element was the *Unità Tecnologica Elementare* (technological elementary unit or UTE), defined as the primary organizational unit that governs a specific segment of the process and operates as a self-sufficient team in managing the processes and resources, monitoring productivity, cost, and performing technology maintenance, continuous quality control, and improvement. Within each UTE, workers were assisted by a team leader whose duties were to improve the quality and training of operators. The main objective of the UTE was to identify and resolve production problems where they manifest and as early as possible: The worker was thus required to identify the first signs of malfunction, to directly verify the application of production standards and make improvement suggestions. The suggestion system enabled workers to offer improvement suggestions (which were then evaluated and potentially applied and remunerated) through quality circles (as described earlier) that operated outside working hours. Each UTE represented a segment of the production value stream and were linked by a relationship similar to that established with suppliers. Each unit worked on the basis of a flow of information provided by the production planning division and supported by charts and indicators on quality, cost, productivity of the product, and process (management by sight system).

New professional figures were introduced: drivers of integrated processes and operators of integrated processes with the role of training workers and undertaking prevention and quality information activities. Teamwork within UTE, however, constituted the fundamental element of this revolution: The UTE/team based organization enabled the hoped-for integration as the name integrated factory suggests, and enabled flexibility and cost reduction.

The quality program and the attempt to learn the Toyota production system described so far was applied with different approaches and outcomes in some Fiat plants in Italy and abroad. The most complete application was in the greenfield Melfi plant, which for a while became the "model factory." The application was later extended to other assembly plants in Italy and Latin America but was more partial and complex in the brownfield factories and in the motor and mechanical manufacturing plants.

Various reasons contributed to slowing down and halting the spread of the Fiat auto production system. Among these, the change in the environmental conditions with the increasing globalization of the automotive industry and new and emerging challenges related to competitive consolidation processes (these were the years of alliances and mergers, such as Daimler-Chrysler and Nissan-Renault). In particular, the organizational transformation based on the Lean Thinking principles had ups and downs in the Melfi plant (Pulignano, 1999, 2000; Lanzara and Patriotta, 2007), producing controversial results, also due to the divided and contradictory positions of the trade unions. In essence, many of the changes advocated by the Romiti plan were implemented only in part or in a different way than expected to the Lean Thinking principles and techniques. Significant results were obtained here and there in terms of improved productivity (reduction in labor hours per vehicle) and quality (reduction of defects in accordance with internal standards and external bodies, such as JD Powers) but with great variance depending on the production context. A problem also emerged that then became somewhat systematic in all the lean transformations of large multinational groups, namely, going beyond episodic or punctual improvements toward sustainable results over time. This was, in the meantime, conjugated with worsening market and financial performance, the supervening implications of the agreement with General Motors (Fiat and GM signed an alliance in 2000 and created two joint ventures for purchasing and powertrain; Camuffo and Volpato, 2002), the expectations of mergers and confluence in the American group, and by the difficulty of continuing and expanding the transformation at the level of business processes upstream of assembly (new product development, supply), downstream of these (marketing), and especially in the organizational structure and managerial behaviors (Volpato, 2007).

In conclusion, many elements suggest that the first attempt at lean transformation in Fiat obtained partial results. The main reasons are probably due to the underestimation of the universal implications from the management perspective of the adoption of the Lean Thinking principles and techniques. If the transformation of product development, production and supply chain processes were clearly pursued through the application of the principles and tools of Lean Thinking, no equal innovation took place in the management system. Fiat experimented and adapted many of the techniques of the Toyota production system and also attempted to transform the operational processes and workers in these activities with massive investments in training, but the management system proved much more difficult to change (Pichierri, 1994). The Melfi plant was an experiment and in some ways a single model that served as reference for other production entities, especially when, with the launch of the Palio World Car, the production structures outside Italy were enlarged and transformed (Camuffo, 2004). Functioning as a template to replicate makes it difficult to assess how it was really applied and extended to the level of the entire business system (moreover, as Melfi was a greenfield plant, it would be very difficult to use this experience as a template for other brownfield plants). In my opinion, the Italian system of industrial relations, which for a long time was stuck in an ideological position, contributed to not improving and extending the experiments of the Melfi experience, so much so that the most relevant innovations and the most interesting applications of the new production model that gradually replaced that of the integrated factory and Fiat auto production system, which as mentioned is world class manufacturing, often took place in foreign settings initially, for instance, in Poland and Brazil (Camuffo and Massone, 2001) and now in the North American Chrysler plants, where the unions have been more proactive and collaborative.

Today, the production system in force in the factories of all Fiat Group companies (FCA, FPT, CNH, Iveco, Magneti Marelli, etc.) is World Class Manufacturing, a very structured system, developed over time by Haime Yamashina based on different theoretical contributions (Schonberger, 1986), including the content of the Toyota Production System and articulating this in a structured and analytical construction of instruments, pillars, and implementation phases.

This is not the place to go into the content, logic, and critical aspects of the production system under FIAT (Fortunato, 2008, 2012; Tuccino, 2011; Volpato, 2011), but the fact that it has found application in many international companies in different sectors seems to demonstrate its validity.

2.3.4 In the Wake of Fiat...

In the wake of Fiat and group companies, several Italian firms (especially large), including Merloni, Pirelli, SKF Italia, and the Zanussi-Electrolux group, started lean programs in the '90s (Cerruti, Ferigo and Follis, 1996; De Toni and Tonchia, 1996). These companies developed models similar to that of Fiat, emphasizing the technological applications of lean tools (TPM, SMED, etc.) and other lean-related aspects of organizational design in their production units.

SKF Italia (ball bearings) in the early '90s began an organizational restructuring process called production channeling. It began with the Villar Perosa plant in Piedmont and then expanded to other production units, such as Bari. Production channeling consists of establishing elementary organizational units called "channels" (the functional equivalent of UTE in FIAT). Precisely as if they were small production units, all the manufacturing stages within these, from raw materials to the finished product, were transformed in a continuous flow. For the SKF Group, the channels formed the basis of achieving the level of quality and manufacturing flexibility needed to meet customer demand and was the starting point of the application of the Lean Thinking principles and techniques. This channeling led to a real physical reconfiguration of the plants. The channels correspond to value streams and small semiautonomous factories with their own resources managed by a single group of people (team) under the guidance of a single channel grouping manager. The teams have the task of pursuing the objectives of quality, productivity, service, and costs of their own channels. In substance, the channels were envisaged as small production units with a high degree of vertical integration and automation within which installation conductors had the task of undertaking the assigned installations and performing quality control while the operators, that is, skilled workers, also provided technical and operational support to colleagues in managing the variances. The channel was thus configured as a minifactory in which workers were organized as cross-functional teams: The ultimate goal was to relocate and integrate all functions and professional resources needed for production management. The channel was the technological basis on which to graft the reorganization, in theory according to the principles of Lean Thinking, which took place under the guidance of Luciano Lenotti from 1994. The lean production program adopted by SKF Italia had some particular elements:

1. At the model level, there was initially a low degree of specification of the organizational design as it was not defined as a new organizational structure, and it was later decided to design it as an adaptive response on the level of the shop floor reorganization.
2. Staff training was emphasized and conceived as a vehicle for organizational change because it constituted the means for defining the job role: The structure of the tasks of professional roles was subject to the outcome of workforce training.
3. Teamwork was adopted as a basic principle of the organization of production work. This was in contrast to other companies in which teamwork was an organizational mode reserved for improvement and innovation activities and individual work was still the foundation of production.
4. The functional integration of tasks took place both at the working role level and the team level: The focus was on the creation of multifunctional roles, at the same time ascribing the team the function of integrating the different roles, the level of qualification, the

professional specialization (other companies sought integration especially between specialists on a team level).

5. The approach to the reorganization was experimental: It was first introduced in some production areas and was then gradually extended to various channels. This enabled reducing the concerns and perplexities related to change in light of the previous experiences.

6. The change process took place from the bottom to top: starting from the lower level and gradually proceeding toward the higher levels.

The SKF lean program and its implementation, in the same way as channeling, was not subject to any confrontation between the company and the unions as the management considered the issue its exclusive prerogative and the time was not ripe to involve the unions.

Similarly, in view of rethinking its business model, in 1991 Pirelli (tires) began the introduction of an extensive program for the implementation of total productive maintenance (TPM) to align all the factories of the group with the desired production and quality standards and sharing this strategic orientation by introducing continuous improvement tools primarily aimed at optimizing the use of manufacturing technologies and the involvement of employees. The first plants in which TPM was launched were Breuberg (Germany) and Izmit (Turkey), and the program was then gradually extended to other European and Americans production centers. For each factory, a development scheme was established that included a preliminary stage of training and benchmarking and later stages of activating the pillars of TPM (autonomous maintenance, planned maintenance, quality maintenance, training and education, and focused improvement).

These stages were accompanied by a changes in the plant's organizational structure, which led to the creation of minifactory teams, groups of quality specialists with the task of supervising the activities of operators in autonomous, self-contained organizational units called minifactories. They were able to rely on a staff function that housed a representative from each TPM pillar and managers dedicated to policy deployment. Each representative was given the task of promoting improvement projects using cross-functional teams to create new standards and best practices. All representatives reported to the TPM plant manager, who carried out coordination activities.

Although this was an integrated system, the application of the pillars of TPM took place at different times in different factories, also given the cultural differences related to the countries they were based in. The guideline was to focus on the activities that produced positive results in the short term. However, this did not prevent language barriers and bureaucracy, which developed in correspondence with the improvement projects (and added to the daily practices), curbing the overall implementation of TPM in Pirelli.

The brief descriptions of the SKF and Pirelli cases (but similar considerations can be made for other companies in different sectors, such as Electrolux-Zanussi, which in its Veneto and Friuli plants—Susegana and Porcia—followed a similar path), beyond the results obtained, illustrate some common elements that distinguish this first wave of the systematic application of the principles of Lean Thinking in Italian companies that can be generalized and used as a lesson for current experiments.

The first consists of the reasons that determine adoption which was the need to survive and remain competitive. In the '90s, the automotive industry, the threat was Japanese competition especially in the automotive industry.

A second factor is the complexity of the business models and production systems and the need for individual skills, organizational capabilities, and management systems able to deal with ever changing problems and unimaginable challenges. In the first wave of the application of Lean Thinking in Italy, this aspect was little emphasized and was too focused on copying or applying tools in the belief that these were the definitive solution to all problems. In fact, there was little awareness that Lean Thinking was a holistic management system and that lean tools are means to develop the skills of people and to ensure the entire organization is prepared for change and ready to face and solve problems in order to improve performance.

The development and involvement of people were perhaps the most problematic aspects of the first applications of Lean Thinking in Italy. Indeed, one cannot fail to recognize that these companies understood the importance of involving all individuals in the company, and one can also not fail to recognize that substantial investments were made for example in terms of training. Yet full employee involvement was not accomplished, and not all the implications potentially deriving from the application of Lean Thinking were drawn, especially in terms of organizational design (organization by value stream and overcoming the functional silos approach), job design (work organization and the versatility of workers with related accountability, delegation of decision-making autonomy and training), and industrial relations (especially with regard to the occupational classification systems, flexibility in job assignment, and the definition of working conditions).

These considerations outline the context of Italian companies that first applied Lean Thinking in the '90s. The experiments were mainly in production (and supplier management, fewer instead in the field of new product development) with a strong emphasis on lean tools, namely, on technical improvement tools (JIT, TPM, *kanban, kaizen projects*, etc.) applied to specific areas of intervention. Less was done to change the management system and develop in all business areas structural and long-term changes, and comparatively, less was also done in terms of building the of people capacities and changing the organizational structures.

In summary, the first applications of Lean Thinking in Italy were mainly in large enterprises. These applications were partial, focused on specific instruments (TPM, TQM, etc.) or on versions of TPS or Lean Thinking that emphasized one or a few methodological aspects (in some cases, the least important). In particular, three main streams can be distinguished that emphasize three aspects and are in some way related to the approaches of the more advanced consulting firms at the time:

1. The approach based on TQM and CWQC introduced in Italy by Galgano, which emphasized the issues of quality and problem-solving and the associated instrumentation (PDCA, seven tools of quality, etc.) by developing pioneering applications in Fiat, SNIA, and Merloni.
2. The integrated factory approach developed and introduced in Italy thanks to the collaboration of some Fiat consultants, such as Filippo Martino, that emphasized the organizational aspects (the UTEs and the AGIs in Fiat and Electrolux and the channels in SKF), that is the concept of clustering production activities that constitute production value streams in semiautonomous units responsible for a certain production outcome. This idea recalls the concept of production cells within value streams without, however, drawing the implications in terms of one-piece flow, work standardization in flexible manufacturing cells linked to *takt* time and the level pull logic sustained by supermarkets or FIFO lanes.
3. The TPM and then the WCM approach focused on technological and economical aspects (waste, losses, cost deployment) operationally developed by Hajime Yamashina and applied in companies such as Pirelli, Indesit, and Ansaldo before becoming established in its extended and full version in Fiat.

2.3.5 The Third Phase of Development: Lean Thinking Meets SMEs

To understand the recent evolution of the lean movement in Italy and ana-lyze the application of Lean Thinking in Italy in the 2000s, especially in the first part of the decade, reference can be made to the publications of some consultants who are merited with spreading the principles of Lean Thinking in medium-sized companies that were experimented in larger firms in the preceding decade. Among these publications are those of Alberto Galgano (2002, 2005) mentioned previously in this chapter, sus-taining the need for radical change, a revolution to be undertaken with courage and risk-taking by Italian companies that wanted to survive and return to growth. According to this approach, the three fundamental revolutions to apply the principles of Lean Thinking are: the centrality of the product in the process, emphasizing flows of materials and informa-tion; pulse-line manufacturing in line with market changes, which must involve the entire production structure; rapid and continuous improve-ment, the results of which should become evident and measurable in a few days (in terms of waste reduction). Then, as now, few SMEs have really completed comprehensive lean transformations. A larger number of SMEs have experimented with lean tools and in some cases undertaken true lean transformation processess. However, only recently the speed and extent of the spread is such as to have a visible impact. As elsewhere in the world, many Italian SME owners, entrepreneurs, and managers still remain estranged or reluctant to approach the new model either because they are unaware of it or because they do not consider it necessary for their busi-nesses. Thus, at this stage, the diffusion of Lean Thinking remains modest (a rough estimate suggests that only 1% of Italian companies belonging to Confindustria, the Italian manufacturers' association, has tried to adopt some of the Lean Thinking techniques) and few (excluding the honorable exceptions mentioned in this book) can be considered successful or exem-plary instances of the type that in the meantime have become affirmed around the world.

Similar considerations were proposed by Bonfiglioli (2001, 2006) who a decade ago stated, "...it is not enough to talk about something (lean) to be able to claim to have done it. Companies that say they implement Lean Thinking have often patchily applied lean production: flow lines that pro-duce for a finished goods warehouse... without *takt* time, without fraction-ing, without involving suppliers..."

As highlighted in Chapter 1, this conclusion is paradoxical in the sense that, although for many other decisions or strategies Italian SMEs' owners, entrepreneurs, and managers have a number of justifications at their disposal related to the unfavorable conditions of the context or the lack of resources to finalize investments, in many cases the application of the Lean Thinking principles and techniques is not capex intensive, that is, it does not require massive investments in fixed capital but few and profound investments in intellectual and organizational capital in terms of knowledge and organizational processes.

Compared to the '90s and the situation described by Galgano and Bonfiglioli, two very significant changes have given a boost and a different direction to the Italian lean movement in the last decade. The first is a development in the degree of understanding the determinants of the success of companies that adopt the principles and tools of Lean Thinking. The second is an evolution of the competitive and economic institutional environment in which Italian SMEs operate.

With respect to the past, previously unexplored aspects of Lean Thinking have emerged or been clarified. In particular, (a) the fact that these are not production–engineering techniques relegated to the management of production and logistical flows and plant resources; (b) the fact that the application of the Lean Thinking principles and techniques requires reviewing the company's organizational perspective toward a nonfunctional, value stream–based approach and are applicable to all business areas and processes from new product development (Liker and Meier, 2007; Ward and Sobek, 2014) and information systems and IT (Bell and Orzen, 2010) to administration and human resource management (Keyte and Locher, 2004; Liker and Hoseus, 2008); (c) the fact that the application of the Lean Thinking principles and techniques requires the adoption of a holistic approach and the involvement of customers and suppliers along the supply chain with a view to the extended enterprise and the extended value stream (Jones and Womack, 2011); (d) the fact that the application of the Lean Thinking principles and techniques is through the adoption not of a set of solutions but a set of learning routines that nurture problem-solving skills and thus improve the organization in the face of different problems (Fujimoto, 1999; Shook, 2008; Anand et al., 2009; Rother, 2009); and (e) the fact that some specific managerial behaviors, especially if disseminated at all levels, make these routines real improvement and learning processes rather than bureaucratic and superstructural activities and artifacts (Seddon, 2005; Dennis, 2006; Jackson, 2006; Liker and Franz, 2011; Liker and Convis, 2012; Mann, 2014).

The second change concerns the global, national, and local economic and social context in which Italian SMEs operate, changes faced by SMEs around the world. During the last 10 years, this context was first affected by competitive pressure from countries with lower labor costs, particularly China, and the temptations to outsource or relocate production to take advantage of these lower costs. Companies that made the decision to move production offshore initially enjoyed significant advantages, but when not sustained by robust business models, sound market positions, and innovative product and process technologies, they soon saw their margins eroding as well as the market shares temporarily reconstituted with delocalization. In sum, transient short-term advantages that soon disappeared because the lower unit cost of production obtained with relocation often did not correspond to the reduction of the total cost of ownership of the product and instead corresponded to greater logistical, contractual, and financial risks. Conversely, as evidenced by some of the cases described in Chapter 1, some more forward-looking SMEs, instead of choosing the low road of relocation and making life easier through offshoring and/or outsourcing, chose the high road to maintain production and employment in Italy and tried to climb up the difficult path of improving productivity and increasing competitiveness through the adoption of the Lean Thinking principles and techniques. Even here, however, some SMEs have gone only partially down this road, mainly operating on the production processes and trying to obtain specific and immediate improvements in productivity, efficiency, and quality through the application of the Lean Thinking principles and techniques. Other businesses, however, such as those described in Chapter 1, have embarked on a path of total transformation, adopting the holistic approach mentioned earlier, at the same time calling into question the business model, the relationship with the market, and the innovation and production processes. These lean transformations proved to be much more effective and have in common (a) the strong leadership role of the owner/entrepreneur and (b) the adoption of Lean Thinking suitably adapted and modified, not as an instrument of production efficiency but as a philosophy and overall management system.

When, in the second half of 2008, the entire world economy entered into crisis, the competitive and market environment of Italian SMEs was further aggravated, creating additional problems, often even in terms of their survival. In general, as I will show in Chapter 5, companies that had already undertaken lean transformations reacted better than others, especially those that had—as in the cases described in Chapter 1—(a) radically rethought the business model; (b) foreseen specific investments in the acquisition and development of lean capabilities; and (c) understood the link between a management system based on Lean Thinking, measuring company performance, and financial and debt structure/dynamics.

Many other SMEs instead started too late to transform as a result of the crisis. In many of these cases, attempts to apply the Lean Thinking principles and techniques either produced episodic improvements or were not effective and were unable to save the companies in question.

Overall, there is now greater awareness in Italian SMEs of the potential of Lean Thinking. In many cases, this has derived from its spread along the supply chains by force of large national and multinational customers requiring its adoption in Italian suppliers. Alternatively, lean transformations have been triggered by imitating, especially at the local level, pioneering and more advanced companies and the flourishing conference, training, and consultancy initiatives often facilitated or led by local business associations.

Not to be underestimated are also the effects related to the acquisition of Italian companies by multinationals. In these cases, the "contamination" and the spread of Lean Thinking has not been conveyed by way of contracts and business relationships or through elevating the performance standards required by the international customers of Italian SMEs. This process occurred instead through equity-type vehicles, exposing and hybridizing the local management and business operations with Lean Thinking introduced by new shareholders or by new ownership.

An interesting case in this regard is the Italian factory of Rexnord whose lean transformation story is discussed in Chapter 4.

2.4 GIOVANNI'S TIRES

I met Giovanni Pomati when he was already senior vice president of Pirelli. In 25 years with the company, he experienced all the transformations while covering an impressive array of roles in the industrial and logistics divisions up to becoming director of global operations.

Thanks to this experience, Giovanni is also a privileged witness of the last two developmental stages of the lean movement in Italy described in the preceding sections.

A management engineer having graduated from the Polytechnic of Milan in 1989 with a thesis based on an internship at the Bollate plant, Giovanni worked for a time in Milan and then began a six-year experience at the Breuberg factory in Germany covering various positions from managing improvement projects to plant director. Backed by the experience in Germany, at that time a pioneering center of excellence in the application of TPM, Giovanni returned to Italy in 1998 and spent a year relaunching the former Vettura plant in Settimo Torinese and then became director of the industrial vehicle business unit. After a spell in the logistics department, in 2004 he was appointed head of Industrial Car Europe. Giovanni then became director of global operations at Pirelli, a position he held between 2009 and 2012, and today he is corporate development and diversified business SVP and new Pirelli industrial project leader.

The professional experience of Giovanni is of particular interest to the Italian lean movement as it reflects its evolution as outlined in the previous sections.

Having come into contact with the most "industrial" interpretation and technology of the Toyota production system that has its roots in the work of Shigeo Shingo and in the development of the TPM and SMED techniques, in Breuberg Giovanni experienced the aforementioned second phase of development. At this time, the equation between competitiveness and the Japanese model reigned, and the most important element was learning the techniques and knowledge as well as developing a sufficient number of specialists able to apply them. In particular, Pirelli had staked everything on the implementation of TPM with the support of EFESO Consulting and (the fierce factory audits) of Jaime Yamashina.

At Breuberg and in the various subsequent experiences in Pirelli, Giovanni also applied many other Lean Thinking tools, particularly those relating to problem solving and quality, putting them into practice in the first person. Among the most interesting is the use of the A3 tool that at the time was little known in Italy. Giovanni still keeps (and proudly shows) his first A3, developed almost 20 years ago under the supervision of Yamashina. However, it was only with the appointment as senior vice president of operations (and reading—as he himself pointed out—the book by Alberto Galgano *Toyota. Perché l'industria italiana non progredisce* [*Toyota. Why Italian Industry Does Not Progress*]) that Giovanni gradually adapted his conception of Lean Thinking from a set of production techniques to a production management system, formalizing this adaption in the Pirelli manufacturing system, a production system characterized by balancing instruments and people in the pursuit of improved production performance in Pirelli factories around the world.

This system was the result of a long process undertaken by the Pirelli senior operations management team via successive approximations while, in turn, conducting a series of experiments in the field in different plants: 5S, supermarkets and *kanban*, VSM and problem solving based on A3 were introduced in the factories in Slatina (Romania), Santo André, Bahia (Brazil), and Breuberg (Germany), while the Settimo Torinese plant was completely restructured and reorganized becoming an international benchmark. Pirelli spared no investments in lean capabilities from training to consulting (with Shingijutsu among others).

Following the experiences of Giovanni and Pirelli has been a little like conducting a social experiment. In a large, complex, global company with a long industrial tradition and endowed with a team with great industrial capabilities, I have been able to witness over the years virtually all the problems typical of the lean transformation process being addressed.

A first example, and I remember the long evening discussions at the headquarters of Pirelli in Milan, was the choice of the degree of codification of PMS, the degree of centralization of its implementation, and the role of the headquarters in rolling it out in factories around the world. Use a unique system designed centrally and spread it to the plants? What degree of autonomy should the plants have in interpreting the system? How much central support should be provided? These are key questions faced by all multinational groups that Giovanni and Pirelli, also based on previous experiences of implementing TPM, responded to by deciding that the center had to provide the guidelines, principles, and support but leave plenty of space to the plant management to experiment, to find the "proper way" of implementing PMS, and favoring horizontal exchange, interplant comparisons in the logic of *yokoten* (best practice sharing). In this sense, it was somewhat exciting to watch how a recent factory (with a young industrial team) such as Slatina in Romania represented the best practices of the group with regard to the implementation of 5S.

A second example concerns the speed with which the principles and concepts of Lean Thinking were applied in the startup of new factories, such as in China and more recently in Russia and Mexico. I particularly remember the discussions with Giovanni on using Slatina as a model factory in which to train the Mexican staff on the potential use of TWI techniques so that the start of the Mexican plant would be faster and more effective.

A third example concerns the vocational practice of Pirelli's industrial management and the strong results orientation. Even for industrial directors, training about Lean Thinking was almost held in the shopfloors following an experiential, learning by doing. A *gemba* walk during the night shift at the factory in Slatina was particularly memorable as was the discussion on the application of the Lean Thinking techniques in the vulcanization molds.

Giovanni is, as other people that I have mentioned in this chapter, an example of evolution and adaptability, a manager who—thanks to a personal, two decade–long lean journey—discovered that his role is to train others to teach Lean Thinking so that they leave their comfort zone and enter into the learning mode (Rother, 2009), which enables being more rational, more able to see problems and solve them, and to perceive the risks and avoid them.

2.5 UNDERSTANDING THE CONTEXT OF LEAN TRANSFORMATIONS

As already mentioned, the Italian lean movement started late and for a long time was very difficult and thwarted. Although the first experiments (first developmental stage) date back to the second half of the '70s and '80s, the phenomenon that came from overseas took more than a decade to find systematic, concrete, and conscious applications first at Fiat and then at a few other large companies often linked to the automotive sector. Since 2000, the slow and opposed adoption of the Lean Thinking principles and techniques has been one of the ways through which Italian SMEs tried to provide an answer to endogenous decline and, in particular, to the dramatic drop in productivity and in the relative international competitiveness. The lines of development of the lean movement in Italy differ greatly by geographic region, industries, and business categories. Understanding these differences is important to contextualize any attempt to transform and realize the enabling and inhibiting factors, the networks, and the resources available to undertake a lean transformation. Unfortunately, as in all the other countries, no reliable data and information is available on the past and current penetration rate of Lean Thinking in Italian SMEs, yet. All in all, from existing anecdotal evidence and expert estimations, SMEs that have at least adopted some lean tools are still a small fraction on the whole although awareness of their existence and the level of knowledge have increased significantly over the past 10 years.

A recent study I conducted on the frequency and content of articles on Lean Thinking in the Italian business press (Camuffo, 2014) provides an indicator, although very approximate, of the levels of experimentation taking place. In the absence of firsthand data, the underlying assumption is that coverage by the financial trade press is a reasonable proxy for estimating the extent to which the experimentations are in some way meaningful. In the Italian case, I analyzed the database of *Il Sole 24 Ore*, the most authoritative Italian financial newspaper. An analysis of the articles on Lean Thinking published since 1990 shows some interesting regularities.

The first consists of an upward trend over time with two frequency peaks, one between 1993 and 1997 and one between 2009 and 2013. These peaks correspond roughly to two (second and third) of the three developmental stages of the Italian lean movement discussed in this chapter.

The second consists of a prevalence of diffusion in large companies during the 1993–1997 period (the second stage of development of the Italian lean movement) and a prevalence of diffusion in SMEs in the 2008–2012 period (the third evolutionary phase of the Italian lean movement).

The third concerns the sectoral concentration. In the first wave, the businesses were concentrated in the automotive and mechanical sectors, and later adoptions gradually spread to other sectors (such as furniture and interiors) and, most recently, services.

The fourth concerns the geographic distribution of the Italian lean movement. Businesses in the northeast mastered it in both the second and the third stage of development, confirming that this is the more lively and dynamic entrepreneurial geographic area in Italy.

The results of this analysis confirm the evolutionary path of the Italian lean movement illustrated in this chapter. The articles analyzed, all covering in various capacities news on the application of the Lean Thinking principles and techniques in Italian companies, provide a first full picture, although clearly an approximate and conservative estimate, of the spread of Lean Thinking in Italian SMEs and the spread of the lean movement in Italy. The data confirm two major phases of development in the evolution of the application of the Lean Thinking principles and techniques in Italy from the beginning of the '90s to the present:

1. A phase corresponding to the second phase of development outlined in this chapter, which began in the early '90s and saw Fiat as its protagonist and a few other large companies, such as Pirelli, Zanussi, and SKF Italia. The initial spread of the lean movement centered on the production of motor vehicles and then contaminated the Italian mechanical engineering industry. However, after the mid-'90s, the number of articles decreases, which could be an indication of either less press attention to the movement and the experiments or may actually correspond to the passing of the managerial "fashion." After becoming popular in correspondence with the rise in Japan and Japanese companies, and in particular Toyota's achievement of competitive supremacy in the automotive industry (with the relative imitation processes also triggered in Italy), the Lean Thinking experimentation slowed and gradually lost force in the absence of specific strategic and competitive motivations.

2. A phase corresponding to the second phase of evolution outlined in this chapter, which started at the beginning of the 2000s but culminated in the 2008 post-crisis years, during which, on one hand, large companies now belonging to new sectors (re)discovered the principles of Lean Thinking, and on the other hand, SMEs began experimenting with Lean Thinking. The factors that led to these new experiments were related to globalization and localization. Globalization, through the need to adapt to the demands of the highest standards of productivity and quality of international industrial customers (many of whom were also involved in lean transformation processes) pushed companies in their international supply chains or otherwise exposed to international competition to launch the application of the Lean Thinking principles and techniques in order to maintain and/or develop the business. Delocalization (especially in China) forced Italian companies (especially SMEs) that were unable or did not wish to move production to countries with low labor costs to launch the application of the Lean Thinking principles and techniques to regain competitiveness in terms of production costs. These strategic reasons, as exemplified by the case studies presented in the second chapter, were progressively modified over time. In particular, firms that started applying the Lean Thinking principles and techniques after the second half of 2008 did so for reasons of survival, often in an attempt to restore the deficits in their financial accounts and their positions as a result of the crisis.

This chapter intended to provide some insights about the context in which Italian SMEs have applied Lean Thinking. As in most other countries, the diffusion of Lean Thinking and the quality of its application are difficult to quantify. For SMEs, understanding what is the degree of maturity of a country's Lean movement is important to exactly know what type of resources and capability are locally available to successfully undertake and sustain a Lean transformation. As the description of the evolution of the Italian Lean movement has shown, the level of awareness, knowledge, and training and consulting services availability is time dependent. Furthermore, the diffusion of Lean Thinking across industries and companies is nonlinear and contingent on institutional and economic variables. In general, contextualizing is important for SMEs' owners, entrepreneurs, and managers who have undertaken lean transformations or wish to do so. It can help to understand what to do (and what not to do) and how to do it.

Chapter 5 will develop this analysis, focusing on the evolution of the financial performance of a large sample of Italian SMEs that have truly undertaken lean transformations and on its determinants.

3

How to Transform SMEs

3.1 THE LEAN TRANSFORMATION FRAMEWORK

The success stories told in Chapter 1 provide an original perspective on lean transformations in small and medium-sized enterprises. The most surprising aspect is that, by adopting Lean Thinking, they all underwent complex organizational changes, not simply restructuring and cost reduction. Moreover, despite the different sectors, sizes, ages, and business models, these cases are characterized by five common elements that also provide a first set of guidelines on how to successfully undertake lean transformations in small and medium enterprises.

The first common element is the fact that in the cases analyzed the owner, entrepreneur, or managing director had a clear idea of the strategic problem he had to solve in order to survive and thrive. Very often, Lean Thinking is used as a "toolbox" to reduce costs without first clarifying the strategic challenges to be faced and then questioning the company's strategy. Lowering costs is pointless if a company's product or service does not meet the actual needs of customers or does not do so in a different way than the competition. Indeed, "efficiency" or "streamlining" may even accelerate or exacerbate critical business issues. In the cases narrated, Lean Thinking is adopted as a philosophy and a discipline that is not only inseparable from resolving the strategic problem but allows effectively defining the strategic goals through the rigorous application of *hoshin kanri* (or strategy deployment).

The second common element is the fact that the transformation processes underlying the application of the Lean Thinking principles and techniques have resulted in substantially changing the business processes and, as a result, improving operating performance. In all cases analyzed, one or more business value streams were significantly revised, changing the constituent activities by applying concepts such as *takt* time, one-piece flow and pull, modifying the organizational structure from functional to value stream–based, engaging people and changing incentive systems, and adopting rigorous and shared problem-solving techniques.

The third element is the systematic presence of substantial and specific investments in people's capability and lean knowledge. In all the cases illustrated, a decision was made to acquire specific skills, to design and implement training programs, to organize education and training centers, and to structure internal learning and/or knowledge transfer units, resulting in strengthening the human capital and more specifically in building capabilities in areas such as value stream mapping, problem solving based on A3, standardized work, TPM, SMED, VOC, and so forth.

The fourth common element is the existence of a clear management system and leadership. All entrepreneurs in the companies analyzed not only did not obstruct the process of change, sponsoring and funding it, but they became the real internal champions of the project, the *sensei* who taught others how to implement and operate according to the principles and practices of Lean Thinking. The lean transformation processes appear to be efficient on the condition that the first transformation takes place at the individual level, not only in terms of language and management techniques, but also in terms of leadership and managerial behaviors.

Also, all the cases are characterized by a management system—that is, a set of shared rules about how to gather evidence, surface problems, define priorities, achieve consensus on courses of action, and monitor progress toward goals. Throughout the transformation process, the entrepreneurial and managerial roles were clear, particularly with regard to sponsoring the transformation process from its launch, assigning responsibilities for stabilizing and improving processes, and designing and managing teams.

The fifth element is sharing a common business philosophy and organizational culture consistent with the principles of Lean Thinking. The analyzed transformations are all permeated by values such as respect for people, consistency of behavior, intransigent respect for rules, anchoring decisions to facts and empirical evidence, and operational involvement of everyone.

These five common elements are the "ingredients" needed to successfully transform a small business as well as a framework to be used as a guide for those who really want to undertake a lean journey.

This framework, shown graphically in Figure 3.1, offers a situational or contingency approach to lean transformations and should therefore be interpreted according to the business. Originally developed by John Shook at the Lean Enterprise Institute, the lean transformation framework (LTF)

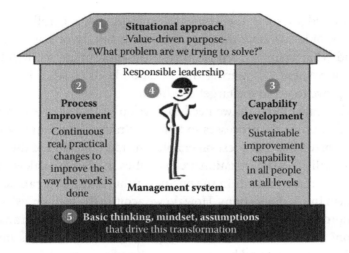

FIGURE 3.1
The Lean Transformation Framework. (Courtesy of Lean Enterprise Institute, http://www.lean.org/WhatsLean/TransformationFramework.cfm.)

has been extensively used to solve business and strategic problems particularly by the affiliates of the Lean Global Network, including the Italian Istituto Lean Management.

The lean transformation framework consists of five basic questions that each SME owner, entrepreneur or manager must ask and periodically re-ask and which must be answered together with their own coworkers. Here are the five questions:

1. What is the strategic problem we are trying to solve?

   SME Business owners, entrepreneurs, and managers need to question the ultimate goal of the lean transformation they have undertaken or wish to undertake. Asking this question leads to defining the target condition and allows the clarification of the real motivations to transformation and link it to the strategic goals. An ancillary question to this is what measures enable us to understand if this strategic problem is resolved or being resolved? This is also extremely important as the way in which it is answered allows problems to surface, and you can monitor progress against the goals.

2. What processes and work do we need to improve in order to solve the strategic problem, and how do we improve them?

   It is important to appropriately choose which value streams need to be improved and what level and type of improvement must be achieved to solve the strategic problem. As a corollary, managers should ask how the improvement is taking or has taken place and what value stream measures are appropriate to monitor this improvement. Answering this question leads to what is needed to improve to get to the target condition.

3. What capabilities do we need to develop so that people can operate and improve the processes so that the strategic problem is solved?

    Answering this question enables the identification of the individual skills and organizational capabilities needed to achieve the necessary improvements in the business value streams. It can be broken down into subquestions: How do we acquire the lean knowledge and improvement capabilities necessary to undertake the transformation? How do we develop the capabilities of all workers involved? What resources and learning model best fit our needs?

4. What management system and leadership is in place?

    This question is intended to assess what role the SME owner, the entrepreneur, and/or top managers have and if their responsibilities and areas of activity are clear. In addition, it regards how they behave and what mechanisms are in place about how to collect information in order to grasp the situation, detect abnormalities, define priorities, gather consensus on decisions and courses of action, allocate resources, and monitor progress toward goals. What managers do is extremely important as it informs the way the whole organization functions.

5. What is the basic thinking of the organization?

    This question has to do with the assumptions underlying how people think and what people do on matters such as the nature and preference of human beings, what is right or wrong, time orientation, and the role of science and technology in human endeavors. Asking this question leads to understanding what thinking style and culture exist and what approaches are needed to change the basic thinking and spread learning.

The stories told in Chapter 1 as well as many others of lean transformation in Italian SMEs suggest that business owners, entrepreneurs, or top managers who, together with their teams, periodically question themselves in a serious and disciplined way on these five aspects of their lean journey have a higher probability of successfully transforming their company.

The answers will always differ, not only among companies, but within companies, depending on the stage of maturity of the transformation process. For example, the emphasis will be on improving operational processes or developing skills and organizational capabilities, depending on the strategic problem, its severity, or the SME owner's temporal orientation. Similarly, underlining some of the values of Lean Thinking, such as incremental improvements, standardization, the scientific approach to problem solving, differs depending on the competitive, institutional, technological, and social environment in which the company operates.

Also, the leadership needed to initiate a lean transformation in a struggling company will differ from what might be more appropriate to sustaining lean efforts in a successful small business.

The following sections in this chapter, after having summarized some basic Lean Thinking concepts, offer the reader some thoughts and suggestions on how to operationalize this framework, effectively respond to the questions underlying it, and successfully lead a lean transformation.

3.2 CHOOSING THE STRATEGIC PROBLEM TO BE SOLVED

3.2.1 A Matter of Strategy

In practice (and sometimes in theory), two mistaken beliefs are often associated with Lean Thinking. The first is that lean transformations are based on a set of managerial tools independent of the system of organizational relationships within the company and the quality of those working therein (the social system). This belief, unfortunately entrenched and widespread, leads to overestimating the impact of the application of the Lean Thinking tools on business results and overlooks the social and organizational costs of the failure to involve people.

The second is that lean, even if fully and properly conceived as a sociotechnical system (tools and people), is a management system that is independent of the corporate mission and its strategy. This belief, which is unfortunately equally entrenched and widespread, leads management to focus on the wrong things, for example, applying lean tools to "create efficiency" as an end in itself, to support obsolete products or services, to defend an unsustainable market position in relation to competitors, or to legitimize an approximate market approach or customer portfolio with no prospects.

In reality, failing to apply the scientific method (PDCA approach) to resolving the "problem of problems" (i.e., the strategic problem) is a betrayal of the Lean Thinking philosophy even if all other lean tools are applied and the processes have become more efficient.

So, the first question of the lean transformation framework helps us clarify how a small business will create value by identifying the strategic problem(s) we want to solve.

In a context in which SME owners, entrepreneurs, and management are inundated with information and in which competition and uncertainty are more and more intense, companies cannot but continue to call into question their assumptions, their goals, and their action plans in ever more frequent learning cycles that need to be increasingly rigorous and methodologically sound.

Who are our customers? What is of value to them, and what do they really want? What can we offer more of and better than in the past and in relation to the competition?

Survival and success stem from identifying real business opportunities through rigorously listening to the market—the so-called voice of the customer (Campos and Ballad, 2009)—the continuous refinement, development, and verification of the customer's problems we are to solve, as well as of the degree of fit between such problems and the solutions to them we have designed and offer, be they products or services.

The emphasis on customer centricity and value creation rather than on cost reduction enables clarifying some misunderstandings of many lean programs, typical of SMEs, in Italy and around the world.

Doing the things you do better (by adopting lean tools) requires deciding what the "right things to do" are and adopting a robust approach to understanding the market and preparing the offer for customers. In the words of Peter Drucker, who opposed the overly technical and methodological conception of Alfred Sloan on the nature of management, management is a scientifically founded practice wherein the choice of the object (the mission, strategy, objectives, positioning, goal) is not indifferent to the method. Lean Thinking is also and above all this: having a discipline to choose the right things to do and doing them or getting the right things done (Dennis, 2006). Successful small businesses in Italy and around the world always question and re-question what they are doing prior to how they are doing it.

It is by now well known that in the global context a small firm is much more likely to fail and disappear not because it is inefficient but because it is ineffective—that is, because it does not understand the market or serves it the wrong way or does not adapt to the evolving needs of customers. Complementary evidence of this is provided also by the increasingly widespread application of the lean startup method (Ries, 2011; Blank, 2013) in which concepts such as running structure business experiments and frequent changing of products and business models though pivoting lie at the very heart of successful startups.

The underlying assumption of Lean Thinking is that in defining what is of value to the customer, and, hence, the solution to the strategic problem, a hypothesis-driven and evidence-grounded approach, based on discovery-driven planning (McGrath and McMillan, 2009) should be applied. In order to do that, lean thinkers tend to apply a specific methodology, *hoshin kanri* (a term deriving from the Japanese *hoshin* = direction and *kanri* = management). This powerful management tool allows addressing the strategic process as a series of iterative cycles of PDCA in which the business goals are systematically aligned and realigned to the changing market and competition, duly combining through experimentation the analysis of information from the *gemba*, the A3 portfolios at all organizational levels and the performance gaps that occur (Akao, 2004; Jackson, 2006). Using *hoshin kanri* in SMEs allows (a) valorizing the contributions of all firm actors in formulating and executing the strategic objectives (for example, through catch ball); (b) involving all actors participating in the strategic process as carriers of information from the *gemba*, so that top management does not rely solely on the knowledge derived from data and business intelligence in making strategic decisions; (c) establishing the "ground" and a method to explain the diversity of views and assessments to contain unnecessary dissent and conflict, promoting the attainment of consensus (*nemawashi*) through confrontation, critical reflection (*hansei*), and the solution to problems (no compromise or political games); and (d) establishing the strategic process based on information associated with facts (not solely on data), duly updated and immediately useful in making decisions.

Two other aspects are of particular interest to the strategic processes of SMEs in Italy and everywhere else.

The first is the role of the *sensei*, the master supporting the transformation. Those who are familiar with the lean approach know how important it is to have one or more (in the case of larger companies) sparring partners that are able to challenge managers, technicians, and employees (providing inspiration, vision, advice, and raising the bar in terms of goals) and, at the same time, are able to teach through the Socratic method (providing people with support through coaching but without substitution). Certainly, this role can and should be interpreted differently in different small firms and in part as a function of individual differences and in part depending on business needs.

In SMEs, this role could be played either by owners/entrepreneurs, who should ensure continuity and succession rather than operativity, or by the management or consultants, who should, especially the latter, provide support in the critical reflection on strategic and organizational change rather than cater off-the-shelf solutions. However, in both cases, much remains to be done for two reasons. On one hand, SMEs' business owners and entrepreneurs (and this is the best case) cannot resist the temptation to get involved in operations or rely on their own expertise. They tend toward micromanagement and problem fixing rather than training and thus not promoting learning and staff development (including next-generation family members). On the other hand (and this is the worst case), they misinterpret their "managerial" role, distancing themselves from the problems and the organization. Then again, management and consultants—and not always through their own fault—run the risk of offering solutions and episodic and sporadic improvements rather than creating the conditions to facilitate profound transformation processes to produce lasting results.

The second aspect concerns the role of the leader in a lean perspective, which again is much closer to the idea that management is a practice rather than a science. Taking care of a small company presupposes that a business owner, entrepreneur, or managing director subordinates her own interests to the company's ones and that her decisions are based not on opinions, on enforcement, or on personal/family preferences and interests, but only on the strength of evidence and facts.

3.2.2 A Matter of Innovation

Another mistaken belief, perhaps the most subtle and dangerous, is that SMEs' lean transformations are useful and appropriate for firms that do not compete on innovation, seldom develop new product and process technologies, and rarely change their business models.

SMEs that make this mistake believe that the innovation process, and particularly the development of new products and processes, are by their very nature unstructured and "creative" processes and hence not easily adaptable to the principles and tools of Lean Thinking.

From this point of view, Italian companies, and in particular those linked to the Made in Italy rhetoric or to the ideology of "districts" (geographical clusters) or "family entrepreneurship" are in some way exemplary. Indeed, in many cases, they eschew the adoption of structured approaches in the innovation process (especially product innovation) and refuse to follow ordered and disciplined methods in developing products and processes. They often do this in good faith, focusing on the artisanal or semiartisanal tradition of their designers, on the unconditional trust in the genius of the entrepreneur, or on the ability to integrate knowledge and technologies leveraging external sources.

But can we take the innovation capability of SMEs for granted? Are we sure that they would know how to translate research into state-of-the-art technologies and incorporate these in new products and processes that actually meet customers' demand? Products that are not over-engineered and that are quickly and flexibly scalable without requiring reengineering after being launched into production?

Can we assume that these companies would have the capacity to explore what is happening around the world and build alliances, agreements, and research contracts? That they would be able to patent or otherwise protect the intellectual property of new products and processes? That they would be able to identify the financial form and entity best suited to nurturing an innovative idea?

The answer is probably no, and the fact that some of the cases described in the first chapter have instead started their lean transformation from the R&D department and the new product development process are the exception that proves the rule.

Indeed, product development processes are also conceivable as value streams, whose goal it is to develop profitable operational value streams (Ward and Sobek, 2014).

Lean product and process development is based on two fundamental pillars: (a) the process is driven by the end customer, and (b) the principles of Lean Thinking are applied to it. Specifically, it entails (a) creating a flow of activities with the least amount of interruption and (b) standardizing design or planning to reduce variation, create flexibility, and render the results predictable (*henshû kaihatsu* = modularity and *henshû sekkei* = variety reduction program), using visual management tools (*barashi* and visible planning) to align information and behaviors.

In SMEs, product development processes are often out of control with consequent waste, delays, defects, "extra budgets," and problems for industrial and end customers. Lean product and process development can countermeasure these problems as it emphasizes richer and more systematic knowledge generation based on a learning process that Ward and Sobek (2014) define as the LAMDA model (which stands for look, ask, model, discuss, act), a real functional equivalent of the PDCA cycle in the development process of new products. From the organizational point of view, the new product development process in the lean perspective is characterized by four key aspects:

1. Individual entrepreneurship and leadership in projects, namely, the need for a chief engineer who drives the value stream, guarantees customer orientation, and undertakes interfunctional and supplier integration, according to a parallel and not a functional approach (of interest is the use of *obeya*—large rooms in which all the actors of the process come together from the earliest stages of development for the purpose of coordination).
2. The contribution of multiple disciplinary teams, each composed of experts with great technical competencies in the different areas.
3. Set-based concurrent engineering, namely, an evolved version of simultaneous engineering that more effectively and efficiently enables generating and selecting multiple design alternatives, for example, modeling design trade-offs.
4. The application of the concepts of cadence (*takt*), flow, and pull to the design value streams.

Similar to what happens in lean manufacturing in which the by-product of problem solving is the development of skills and people, lean product and process development not only leads to better innovative projects, but also creates knowledge that is reusable and further applicable. The challenge for SMEs is to apply the four above principles despite the scarcity of resources and the variability of the design work.

3.3 IMPROVING THE WORK

3.3.1 Value Stream Mapping and Improvement

Lean Thinking recommends that SME business owners, entrepreneurs, and managers go and see in person to fully understand the situation (*genchi genbutsu*), analyze problems based on direct observation—at the factory, point of sale, etc.—and talk to people.

Although this might seem obvious, as most SMEs are managed so that owners and managers are often directly involved in operational activities, there is more than meets the eye.

Ensuring that *genchi genbutsu* is truly effective requires a structured methodology to spot waste and unnecessary variability in the processes as well as develop an eye for improvement, "learning to see" them. This method is value stream mapping (Rother and Shook, 1999) and, together with A3-based problem solving (Shook, 2008), it allows addressing the second question of the lean transformation framework: What processes and work do we need to improve in order to solve the strategic problem, and how do we improve them?

Value stream mapping and improvement allows representing the actual state of business processes (current state map) to identify waste and critical areas for potential improvement in performance. It also allows to conceive possible future configurations of the value streams (future state map) that are better able to deliver value to customers and indicate the countermeasures and initiatives necessary to accomplish the transition from the existing to a desired/future situation, thus contributing to solving the strategic problem that the SME's owner, entrepreneur, or manager set out to solve.

Value stream mapping (VSM) is a set of methodologies that enable graphically depicting the business value streams. This should not be confused with process analysis or reengineering techniques as it integrates with other lean tools to continuously improve business performance by eliminating waste (Keyte and Locher, 2004; Locher, 2008). A value stream map is a simple graphic representation of all the phases and processes related to the information and material flows that characterize, for example, the production of a product or service from order to delivery to the customer. These graphic representations can be referred to at different times (for example, the current, the past, or the future situation) to foster the awareness of all members of the team working on the actual improvement opportunities.

Value stream mapping and improvement is, among all the lean tools, the most comprehensive and has the greatest implications and scope, as they can be applied in every part of the organization. As such, they enbale the following (Hines and Rich, 1997):

1. Understanding and sharing the operating mode of the current business in terms of customer service via a common graphic-type language

2. Making the business flows explicit and visible, analyzing and solving the problems in a way that enables everyone to recognize the critical aspects and opportunities for improvement

3. Creating value streams devoid of waste and unnecessary variability through appropriate planning rules (for example, operating at *takt* time with one-piece-flow cells or through pull systems with volumes and variety of activities leveled by scheduling only one pace maker process, defining the service level agreement with the customer and the *kaizen* initiatives in the improvement plan)

However, especially in SMEs, the essence of value stream mapping and improvement does not lie in its sophisticated application, but rather in how it becomes a shared approach to understand how the key value streams of a small business operate and a way to envision, support, and plan its improvement.

Learning to map the key value streams of a small business (voice of the customer, product and process development, order to delivery and/or cash, sourcing, customer support, etc.) is especially powerful as it is often possible to directly connect their metrics to strategy deployment and, via value stream accounting, company performance—a luxury large organizations can't afford.

3.3.2 Pursuing Just-in-Time via Flow and Level Pull

The transition to lean production can be interpreted as a real revolution in corporate management and of similar dimensions—if the metaphor is not too far-fetched—to that instituted by Einsteinian physics with respect to Newtonian physics. As in the case of the Law of Relativity, which introduced the time dimension alongside the spatial dimension in interpreting the relationship between mass and energy, the contribution of the father of the Toyota production system, Taiichi Ohno, is also based on introducing time alongside space as a fundamental aspect of management (Ohno, 1988).

The predominant element in mass production is space: scale of operations, lot sizes, large plants, equipment, and dedicated machines. The predominant element in lean manufacturing is time, not only spasmodic attention to throughput time and the relationship between value added and throughput time, but also the use of *takt* time as a fundamental parameter of the interface between organizational units or the organization and the market.

The concept of continuously flowing value streams is the fundamental element of the revolution introduced by lean and translates the time element introduced by the Toyota production system into production and organizational design rules.

Creating flow wherever possible—that is, when resources can be dedicated and are capable, available, and flexible—is the first step in value stream design, once value has been identified from the customer's perspective and once the associated value stream has also been identified. However, as described in the next section, although creating uninterrupted flow, typically through one-piece-flow cells, is the first and best option, pulling via supermarkets and *Kanban*, or FIFO lanes, is the second best option to be applied when the characteristics of demand, the technological constraints, operating conditions, or logistics do not enable continuous flow.

Creating a continuous flow value stream (Rother and Harris, 2001) means designing and operating a production system without interruption, in an orderly way, according to a sequence of operations that create value for the customer, possibly according to a pace agreed upon with customers or, more generally, according to demand. Creating a continuously flowing value stream is the real and ultimate goal of just-in-time, but in reality, fully implementing one-piece flow in complex organizational contexts is an abstraction and a utopia. Indeed, only in the abstract could a production system be conceived in which space asymptotically vanishes (up to making factories, warehouses, and offices redundant because the throughput time from order to delivery of products is so short as to be negligible) because the company produces exactly what the market demands without interruption, errors, and technological and human constraints.

However, as shown by the cases in Chapter 1, the lean production systems of more advanced companies are characterized by at least some value stream segments (sometimes significant) that operate according to the "make one–check one–move on one" logic (Black, 2007) or flexible cells in which one or more operators work according to what is foreseen from the application of standardized work, iteratively performing a complete operating cycle (*chaku-chaku*) whose implementation time remains just below the *takt* time.

In other words, a lean production system consists of, wherever possible, cells that operate at continuous flow connected by controlled amounts of stock (supermarkets) and information signals representing pull (*kanban* or FIFO lanes).

Continuous flow can be created within a cell by the following:

- Assigning the products or services and/or different production stages to self-contained organizational units within which activities flow continuously according to the one-piece-flow approach in order to meet *takt* time
- Identifying, through standardized work (job elements, work sequence, etc.) the basic one-piece-flow work operations and the actual time required to implement them
- Choosing, possibly, technologies that are dedicated, capable, available, and flexible, ensuring that equipment or machine times are compatible with the work content and *takt* time
- Calibrating the staffing of cells and organizing work within these in a flexible way by focusing on the versatility and qualification of operators (introducing standardized work as content—job elements, timing and sequencing work, standard work in process–cross-training workers so that they are polivalent and can perform all the tasks within the cell), ensuring the necessary skills through proper training (training within industry), monitoring skills (visual skill boards), and motivation systems
- Connecting with the internal or external customer and regulating the flow of cells by planning the pacemaker process and reacting in a balanced way to changes in demand

3.3.2.1 Pull as a Horizontal Coordination Principle of Physical and Information Flows

One of the aspects that strikes those who observe the *gemba* of industrial SMEs in Italy and elsewhere—with a critical eye toward improving productivity—is the insufficient attention to materials management and logistics.

This derives from an excessive emphasis on point or local efficiency (equipment, department, office, plant, or warehouse optimization) and the inability to evaluate system efficiency. For example, I recently visited a successful midsize producer of raw and melamine-faced chipboards for the furniture industry that wanted to start its lean journey. A well-managed family business, with state-of-the-art product and process technology, excellent product positioning, and a true drive toward sustainability, the owners took me to a *gemba walk* and were surprised when, comparing the production staff with the number of forklifters and warehouse operators, I asked them if they were in the chipboard or transportation business. They took the provocation and immediately realized that their biggest challenge, in order to solve their key strategic problem (aggressive competition from Spain and Turkey), was to improve the materials flow as this would allow the reduction of both cost and delivery times (service levels).

In many SMEs, an internal logistics culture exists and translates into physical and technological investments in both hardware and software (warehouses, handling systems, ERPs, etc.) yet tends to crystallize traditional approaches rather than foster continuous improvement.

Instead, in cases such as those illustrated in Chapter 1, materials flows are intentionally designed to ensure the continuous flow of value to the customer, applying the principle of (level) pull though the use of *heijunka* boxes, supermarkets, and pull signals, the "studied" maximum reduction of movements and handling, visual tools to facilitate assessing stock levels, reordering and procurement decisions, supplies according to the water spider (or *mizusumashi*) approach, the clarity of logistical paths with one-way systems of internal transport, layout choices subservient to the manufacturing cells, and flow optimization, also applying standardized work and 5S methodologies to logistics staff (Smalley, 2004).

The overall concept that can be drawn from these evolved *gemba* is that of order, brightness, and cleanliness; care and respect for the work of other production units; coordinated efforts toward a common goal; less stress on people and things; and work always carried out with respect for the safety of operators.

Materials management and internal logistic flows in a lean production system in which pull connections—consisting of FIFO lanes, supermarkets, and *kanban*—link cells that operate in continuous flow (linked-cell system [L-CMS], Black, 2007) typically require the following:

1. Identifying the plan for each component (PFEP = plan for every part), deciding what information to include and how to keep the PFEP updated
2. Designing the component procurement supermarket and deciding where to place the component supermarket, how to manage it, and the correct amount and how much space is required to store each component
3. Defining the delivery path and the information management system by deciding how to transport components from the supermarket to

the production areas, how the production departments signal to the components supermarket what and when to deliver, and how to optimize the delivery paths

4. Ensuring maintenance and improvement, deciding which audit system is needed to maintain the lean materials management system performance and how to identify and remove additional waste

3.3.2.2 Combat Waste by Eliminating Variability

One of the most important implications of adopting Lean Thinking in SMEs is the potential impact on economic and financial variables, particularly in terms of working capital and, consequently, on the net financial position.

Many Italian SMEs—the same applies to SMEs around the world—have ventured into lean journeys focusing on the reduction of inventories and stock, attracted by the financial benefits to which this leads.

This focus can, however, be misguided because the reduction of inventory and the consequent improvement in the net financial position should not be the effect of a specific action and a goal in itself. Rather, these should be the result of better planning and control of the production system or a more rational relationship between market demand and supply, between the organization and its environment of reference, and between organizational units within the firm.

Also contributing in this sense is the fact that just-in-time has long been misunderstood as a stockless production or utopic one-piece-flow system.

Stock is one of the seven wastes (Ohno, 1988). However, in any lean transformation, the elimination of waste (*muda*) has to go hand in hand with two other lesser-known but equally important aspects (Liker, 2004), which are (a) eliminating the work overload of people and technology (*muri*) and (b) eliminating unnecessary variability in the production process and in its planning (*mura*).

Excessive or undesired variability (*mura*) as a source of waste (*muda*) and stress on resources and operational processes (*muri*) is often not fully appreciated, especially by SMEs (Smalley, 2004). There are two ways in which excessive variability might hurdle lean efforts in SMEs.

The first way regards the need to stabilize any process before starting to improve it. Many SME business owners, entrepreneurs, and managers, tend instead to almost always jump immediately into the improvement projects geared toward the elimination of waste. Yet, in reality, eliminating waste through continuous improvement cannot take place except in a process that is stable and constitutes the baseline whose performance can be measured. In other words, only with stability and measurability is it possible to formulate and measure improvement, and only stable systems can reliably serve the market.

The second way regards the necessity to design value streams that are devoid of unnecessary variation. Beside standardization, leveling (*Heijunka*) is the principle that allows the reduction of *mura* and consists of smoothing the type and quantity of production over a fixed period of time. For many SMEs, production smoothing at all levels is particularly difficult as people tend to resist the counterintuitive idea that leveling production allows meeting customer demand more efficiently than batching to reduce inventories, working capital and staff, and to shorten lead time throughout the whole value stream.

Leveling (*heijunka*) entails (a) correctly interpreting demand and decomposing variability; (b) choosing the pacemaker process for each value stream (at least in cases in which flow is not synchronized); and (c) learning the different heuristics and algorithms of production smoothing, such as the Monden algorithm (2012) (goal chasing model) and the *heijunka* box (Jones, 2006; Mesut and Elif, 2007).

Overall, the need to reduce unnecessary variability is paramount for SMEs, with which standardization is often not an integrative part of the organizational culture. To satisfy this need, the techniques proposed by the theory of constraints (TOC; Goldratt and Cox, 1984) and the Six Sigma approach can be employed as complementary to lean tools (George, Rowlands and Kastle, 2004).

3.4 DEVELOPING CAPABILITIES

3.4.1 Growing People through Problem Solving

"No problem is a big problem." This slogan—widespread in most lean companies—is often a source of concern for SMEs approaching Lean Thinking for the first time. Business owners, entrepreneurs, and managers find it counterintuitive and paradoxical to say that the real problem for an organization is not finding abnormalities within it; a stable situation is apparently not only satisfying but also desirable for a company. SME leaders, probably even more than managers in large companies, like to be in control and need to reduce the level of (perceived) uncertainty looking for definitive solutions. This tendency is a sort of natural response to human preference for certainty and habit as this allows us to operate cognitively and psychologically in a comfort zone (Rother, 2009).

Clearly, a company beset by instability and problems is not an example to imitate. But an organization that is content with what it has achieved or does not have a method to identify, face, and solve problems is a company destined to regress or, at best, not improve.

The essence of lean is relentless problem identification and solving. Troubleshooting of daily problems is one aspect of this. SMEs differ in the ability to frequently and quickly solve minor problems, but overall and especially in the Italian case, they are good at doing this. What they are less good at is preventing processes from getting worse, degrading, deviating from standards or expectations. This is partly related to ill-designed and -operated value streams (absence of clear standards) and partly to the lack of people capability. This lack of capability is probably even more serious when problems are defined as the need to improve performance, to meet higher expectations as defined by more challenging goals, different customers' expectations, or competitors' improvements. These types of problems are where continuous improvement (*kaizen*) initiatives best apply (*kaizen* events, weeks, etc.; Imai, 1995).

Many SME business owners, entrepreneurs, and managing directors often misunderstand the cause–effect relationship among people capability, problem solving, and performance improvements. In some cases, they wrongly assume that capabilities are in place and that, once decided and appropriately initiated (launch of a "lean program," hiring of a consultant, etc.), problem solving will take place, and performance will improve. In other cases, they wrongly assume that investment in capabilities (training, hiring a consultant or a lean expert, etc.) will translate into problem solving and produce performance improvements.

The fundamental mistake is to decouple performance improvement from capability improvement and think of problem solving as solely either an output of learning or an input to improvements. Instead, these three aspects are strictly intertwined (Spear and Bowen, 1999). Separating them, as often happens in SMEs, slows down the transformation.

This confusion is often the main reason why starting and sustaining continuous improvement is so hard in SMEs, and this is also why asking and re-asking the third question of the lean transformation framework—what capabilities do we need to develop so that people can operate and improve the processes so that the strategic problem is solved?—is so critical for SMEs.

In my experience, the capabilities to be acquired and developed to transform SMEs are of three types. The first is the skills required to actually do the work within value streams according to standards. We will see how training within industry (TWI) might be helpful for SMEs to develop these skills effectively and efficiently. The second is lean skills—that is, knowledge and ability about how to effectively apply lean tools in order to effectively and efficiently operate and improve value streams. The third is the skills required to lead and transform—that is the capability to behave appropriately in order to support and foster the transformation. These three types of capabilities are necessary to successfully transform. They are eventually geared toward ensuring that managers and workers are able to recognize problems, tolerate the associated uncertainty, and tackle them with disciplined methods. Thus, the principle of striving for perfection (Womack and Jones, 1996) is a state of mind in which SMEs' owners, managers, and employees feel comfortable with the idea that problems are opportunities for improvement and that it is good to uncover them at every level. Such a state of mind or growth mindset is opposed to the fixed mindset (Dweck, 2006) and also reflects a flexible conception of human intelligence, a positive attitude toward the ability of people to learn and change.

As problem solving takes place, learning also occurs, and new knowledge is generated that can be used later to solve new problems. Thus, lean transformations are successful if everybody gets used to looking for and identifying new problems that, albeit generating discomfort associated with uncertainty, are an opportunity for improvement.

If this happens, problem solving is a process that not only creates value streams that perform better, but also more capable people who see and solve other problems that, in the previous stage, either did not exist or were not detected. Reaching the future state becomes the new current state, and the problem-solving process can begin again. This is the circular procedural path at the base of the continuous improvement process or *kaizen* (Imai, 1995).

Overall, the stories told in Chapter 1 seem to confirm that SMEs successfully transform themselves when they become the following (Spear and Bowen, 1999):

1. Organizations in which people are a sort of community of "little business scientists" and people operate collectively using some "local" version of the scientific method summarized in the PDCA cycle (Deming's plan–do–check–act)

2. Organizations in which everybody uses a rigorous problem-solving process based on direct observation and data collection
3. Organizations in which managers stimulate employees at all levels to engage in experimentation aimed at improvement

Capability development is therefore an integrative part of any lean transformation.

On the one hand, it requires specific investment to acquire and develop skills about how to lead and work in lean environments and how to operate and improve value streams. Although to a lesser extent than in large organizations, in SMEs such a process of capability development requires dedicated resources and specific processes. As far as resources are concerned, investment in training, support from a *sensei*, and support of lean experts are prerequisites. This is usually accepted, at least in theory, by SME business owners, entrepreneurs, and managers although in practice there is a widespread tendency to undersize this investment or not to consider it a priority. Instead, SMEs often fail to make the most of this investment. For example, transfer of lean knowledge from consultants to managers and workers might break down when initiatives such as *kaizen* events are not integrated in the management system or when training is designed by the human resource department without involving line managers in training needs analysis or when lean specialists operate in a segregated manner from line managers or when managers do not integrate teaching lean and coaching about lean in their role.

On the other hand, capability development is also a consequence of Lean Thinking adoption. In fact, learning is a by-product of lean systems because, aside from the main and obvious outcome of improving processes and reducing waste, the adoption of lean practices *concurrently* facilitates the development of people skills in their professional, relational, and organizational components. In short, a transformed SME is a firm that, while systematically resolving problems and improving performance, enables people to learn how to solve them.

3.4.2 A3: Develop Others through Structured Problem Solving and Management without Authority

Most Italian SMEs undergoing successful transformations make extensive use of A3-based problem solving. The A3 methodology (the name derives from using an A3 sheet of paper appropriately structured for collective problem solving) was developed by Toyota for the widespread application of the PDCA method (plan–do–check–act)—that is, problem solving based on the scientific method.

The underlying insight is that people within organizations need to follow a structured, rigorous, and shared problem-solving process, making it possible to appropriately define the problem, identify its root causes, propose a number of possible countermeasures, experiment, and verify their appropriateness, all wrapped up in a sheet of paper, the commendation of essentiality that nonetheless is the outcome of deep and rigorous discussion and dialogue.

As mentioned in the previous section, the A3 methodology applies to problems that do not need to be immediately countermeasured and whose complexity is medium to high.

Similar to other lean tools, however, the perhaps latent but most important function of A3 is that of people development.

A3 is a multiple function managerial tool. It takes three basic meanings, which must be understood if SME owners, entrepreneurs, or managers want to engage in a real lean transformation process (Shook, 2008; Sobek and Smalley, 2008).

3.4.2.1 A3 as a Problem-Solving Tool and Methodology

A3 is a simple, rigorous, and standardized tool to address problems, understand their root causes, propose solutions, and monitor their progress. Indeed, it is a simple organizational artifact in which activities are catalyzed according to a standard mode, and the problem-solving process is ordered according to the scientific method (PDCA cycle).

3.4.2.2 A3 as Management Decision-Making Based on Taking Responsibility

A3 is also a process that configures the nature of organizational relationships and shapes organizational roles, decision-making, coordination, and control processes. Problem solving through A3 is a process based on direct observation on discussion and dialogue with the relevant organizational actors, regardless of their position within the organization, the involvement, and conviction of all those participating in the activity (*nemawashi*) and critical reflection (*hansei*) on what has been done. In this context, making decisions is a delicate task that a manager can only exercise when the situation demands it or the conditions exist and not on the basis of a formally assigned role or status. In this sense, A3 is an extremely powerful tool for SMEs as, on the one hand, it helps structure the organization—the lack of which is a typical problem—and on the other hand, it fits the nonhierarchical character, the community values, and the family culture of many of them. From this standpoint, SMEs are in a better position to fit Taiichi Ohno's idea according to which lean organizations are characterized by "kanban democracy" in which authority is called into question as and when needed: authority on demand, just-in-time, pull.

3.4.2.3 A3 as Learning Process and People Development Tool

A3 is also a learning (and teaching) process. In lean organizations, people are the engine responsible for problem solving and continuous improvement. A3 is precisely the process whereby the "double helix of the DNA of lean systems" (developing increasingly better products while also building increasingly better people) come together and reinforce each other (Spear and Bowen, 1999). An organization founded on A3 is an organization that, while making decisions and solving problems to better serve customers through its value streams, improves itself by improving its members thanks to the role of teacher (*sensei*) undertaken by those who have this responsibility. In the A3 process, the "boss" is also and above all a teacher, and the employee is a student who works while learning.

The key implications of the threefold nature of A3 relate to the characteristics of managerial behaviors that should consist of the following (Spear, 2004):

1. Respect for the person and willingness to listen and learn from others; direct observation and management involvement in problem solving at the operational level (*gemba*)
2. Exercising leadership based not on the principle of authority but on that of responsibility; conception of leadership as a learning process in which the leader is a teacher (*sensei*) using the Socratic method (offering questions, not answers)
3. The idea that decisions, actions, and learning must be based on direct experience and on critical exercise
4. Enthusiasm for teamwork aimed at continuous improvements
5. Modesty and humility

In essence, A3 on one side is an organizational routine, meaning an organizational artifact, a standard way of addressing and solving problems with the advantages of simplicity and rigor, dissemination ease, and extensibility across the organization. In this sense, A3 is an element of stability and organizational efficiency. On the other side, A3 is an organizational routine in the sense that, through the conversations, decisions, and actions of those involved in the A3 process, direction and meaning are given to the managerial processes and the organization while promoting learning.

3.4.3 *Ante Litteram*: TWI in Italy

One of the most formidable weapons available to management involved in a lean transformation for the growth and development of people is training within industry (TWI). This lean tool consists of a unique approach to training and education that historically formed the basis of training activities in Toyota. Two features make this approach particularly effective and, as we shall see, a modern *ante litteram* (ahead of its time). The first is that it is rooted in the science of training and in a tangible, practical, measurable learning model directly attributable to the principle of *genchi genbutsu*. The second is its connection with tout-court management and particularly the use of supervisors and department heads as "disseminators" in the logic of multiplication, the pervasiveness, and the thorough sustainability of standardized work learning processes.

Curiously, the history of TWI and its recent successful application also concerns Italian companies, particularly SMEs.

TWI was born in the United States during the second World War as a countermeasure to speed up training the workforce and increase productivity of the defense industry in a critical phase in which the most skilled male workers were taken from production activities and moved to operational locations.

In August 1940, the National Defense Advisory Commission established the TWI Service to "assist production industries to meet their manpower needs by training within industry each worker to make the fullest use of his best skills up to the maximum of his individual ability, thereby enabling production to keep pace with war demands" (Training Within Industry Service, 1943).

The skills required were very technical; consider that the most significant increases in production and productivity were needed in the shipbuilding–aero naval sector.

The training programs were developed and fine-tuned by the best experts in education science, and four of these experts were charged with running the TWI Service. Channing Dooley, Walter Dietz, Mike Kane, and William Conover (collectively known as "The Four Horsemen") designed various training programs that before being widely applied were adequately tested in the field but were never prescribed. Their adoption by businesses was voluntary.

The three training programs designed by the Four Horsemen (called J-programs: job instructions, job methods, and job relations) were standard and based on a training architecture that did not allow deviating. The reasons related to both the underlying philosophy of learning and the conviction—subsequently proven founded even years later—that standardized training was more easily replicable and could be disseminated faster. Indeed, the propagation effect generated by the training of leaders or instructors who, in turn, trained others ("multiplier principle") was remarkable. In just five years, 1,750,650 people participated in at least one of the TWI programs and obtained the related certification.

Surprising results were also obtained in terms of the performance improvements of more than 16,500 manufacturing establishments whose supervisors were trained by the TWI Service instructors: More than half of these establishments declared increases of more than 25% in relation to productivity, efficiency, and quality. These figures refer to September 1945, the date the program ended, and were therefore achieved in just five years after the founding of the TWI Service. These are particularly surprising when considering that every J-program consisted of only 10 hours of formal training. Famous in this sense was a letter sent in 1942 by T. J. Watson Sr., CEO of IBM, to the War Manpower Commission in which aside from giving thanks he extensively praised the TWI Service.

The J-programs were based on a learning and business management philosophy ascribable to two dimensions: (a) the "five needs of supervisors" and (b) the "four-step method," intended for supervisors, widely understood as "anyone who [is] in charge of people or directs the work of others."

According to the studies of the founders of the TWI Service, supervisors have five requirements that must be met in order to best fulfill their role:

1. Knowledge of the work: This consists of information on materials, processes, operations, and end products characterizing one activity with respect to another.

2. Knowledge of responsibility: This refers to the particular situation of a company in terms of internal policies, regulations, programs, and organizational structure.
3. Skill in instructing: This concerns the ability to develop a skilled workforce, leading to the reduction of defects, waste, rework, and breakdowns. The knowledge acquired is thus passed on to others.
4. Skill in improving methods: This means knowing how to use materials, machinery, and labor and effectively eliminating, combining, rearranging, and simplifying the elements of the current work situation. Currently available resources are thus optimized.
5. Skill in leading: This means knowing how to work with people. The results of supervisors depend on their subordinates and thus require knowing how to work with them to avoid the onset of problems and know how to solve them.

The first two needs are knowledge; the rest are skills. The difference between the two concepts is very important because knowledge can be learned by studying or attending classes, and skills are acquired only with practice. For this reason, the TWI Service focused on the last three needs, developing a suitable program for the achievement of each (respectively, JI, JM, and JR). The first two needs were not included among the objectives of the J-programs because they were considered specific to each firm. In fact, knowledge of work and responsibilities differed from company to company and could not have been standardized as part of a program, such as TWI.

The other fundamental dimension of training within industry is the so-called four-step method. This teaching method was developed by Charles Allen (1919) prior to the first World War and is based on a standard process according to the following phases:

1. Preparation during which the instructor seeks to create in the learner's mind a connection between his experience and the lesson to be taught. This step is considered very important to increase the effectiveness of teaching and arouse the interest of learners.
2. Presentation, the aim of which is to lead learners to grasp the concept being conveyed and juxtapose this with what they already know.
3. Application, with which learners put into practice what they have been taught in theory, enabling the instructor to see if they really learned the teachings.
4. Testing, allowing the learners to do the job unaided and implement in practice what they have been taught.

The Four Horsemen, all connoisseurs of this approach, considered it the foundation of TWI and structured each of the programs on this basis.

Essentially, the components of the J-programs constituted a codified organizational learning routine, whose repetition and replication facilitated diffusion. This codification resulted in small blueprints or pocket-sized method cards that supervisors could carry with them and that summarized the program content and phases.

Officially ceased in the United States in September 1945, as it was deemed "no longer necessary," the TWI Service was extended in Japan and Italy as part of the postwar reconstruction efforts.

Although almost everything is known about how TWI was applied in Japan, becoming standard training practice in many firms, including Toyota (Graupp and Wrona, 2006), it is less known that something similar occurred in Italy. In fact, the Marshall Plan after World War II (or ERP = European Recovery Program), in addition to providing material aid for reconstruction, included the spread of TWI to facilitate the qualification of manpower and restart the reindustrialization process. The spread of TWI occurred among SMEs through the activities of productivity centers, such as the Veneto Productivity Center, founded in 1952 in Vicenza, which had as its first CEO the lawyer Giacomo Rumor, later appointed prime minister twice, in the '70s. Larger firms instead introduced it independently, some even on the trade union's initiative. For example, telephone companies that merged with SIP (such as STIPEL) conducted a number of TWI-inspired programs in the '50s for supervisors (e.g., switching assistants and telephone operators).

During the last decade, there has been a renaissance of TWI use in Italian firms, both large and small. The reasons for this comeback are to be found in its complementarity with the diffusion of standardized work and with the fact that, in Italian SMEs, human resource departments are either absent or undersized. At first sight, this might look like a problem, but in reality, it serves as a way to make line managers, especially supervisors, fully responsible to train and grow their own people. And TWI is the perfect managerial routine to do this effectively and efficiently.

But it must be remembered that, similarly to many other lean tools, it was already available but unused, kept in a drawer, a tool that had contributed to the "economic miracle" of the golden years (the '50s and '60s) that Italian SMEs greatly lament today.

3.5. DRIVING THE TRANSFORMATION: LEAN LEADERSHIP AND MANAGEMENT SYSTEM

3.5.1 What Does Top Management Commitment Really Mean?

Well established among the critical success factors of the lean transformation process is the commitment of the top management. This assertion, however, runs the risk of being rhetoric if not clarified. The misconception is in thinking that top management commitment consists of giving the green light to a lean program and not hindering or at least supporting it to provide the resources required for its implementation and to ensure internal "political" support. Instead, as shown in the lean transformation examples discussed in Chapter 1, commitment must be expressed in the total support of the entrepreneur or top management, who should be the real drivers and engines of the process (Boyer, 1996). Their role cannot be limited to supporting (and not hindering) and "sponsoring" an initiative as often misinterpreted in the rhetoric of organizational change but must fully immerse themselves and be involved, becoming the initiators and incessant stimulators. This involves conducting the lean transformation firsthand, setting an example, participating in all the activities of the transformation, and relentlessly communicating, verbally and nonverbally, that "lean is the strategy" (Byrne, 2012). Yet in SMEs, this is only possible if the owners, entrepreneurs, or managing directors themselves have profound knowledge of the principles and techniques of Lean Thinking, and this knowledge comes from direct experience gained firsthand. To be able to be leaders of the transformation process requires first learning the theory and practice of Lean Thinking by putting themselves in the shoes of the *deshi* (disciple). There are no shortcuts.

Leadership of the lean transformation process is also and especially assumed through the establishment of a management team (not just a *kaizen* promotion office or a lean development office) that is aligned with the strategic intent of the entrepreneur and is able to make it happen. Lack of alignment or skills in first-line coworkers is one of the major causes of the failure of the lean transformation process in SMEs. In particular, one of the most critical aspects of leadership in this process is the entrepreneur's ability to identify people who do not help or hinder the path either because they do not believe or understand it or simply because they do not want to change. These organizational actors that Taiichi Ohno (1988) quaintly called "cement heads" must be identified, persuaded to change, and eventually let go under penalty of interrupting the transformation process.

Similarly in the case of Italian SMEs, the role of top management in managing the lean transformation process has proven to be critical in managing relationships with trade unions that can act as a hindering or facilitating factor in the transformation. If the strategic intentions underlying the application of the principles and techniques of Lean Thinking are genuinely aimed at business development and achieving sustainable results and are not against the workers, also in the case of trade unions, this requires involving them and activating confrontation procedures that will allow them to play their role adequately. However, also in this case, agreement spaces may not exist or prejudicial attitudes may prevail toward Lean Thinking. The unions could thus be obstacles that threaten business survival and growth without actually representing the interests of workers. Any compromise or ambiguity that may undermine the transformation process must be avoided.

3.5.2 Building a Management System: Management Standard Work and *Gemba* Walks

One of the management principles of Lean Thinking that is closest to the typical sensibility of Italian SMEs is that of *genchi genbutsu* (Liker, 2004) (*genchi* = the real place, *genbutsu* = the products and real materials), which essentially means going to see firsthand where the activity takes place to precisely understand the situation and the problems.

More generally, the term *gemba* is often used in lean jargon and has become the most popular way to indicate the "field," the place where production, design, sales, or any other activities take place. The principle is to not trust hearsay and financial reporting data but grasp the situation complementing complete information deriving from business information systems with firsthand knowledge that comes from direct observation and from personal conversations with operators and middle management.

This is one of the management principles of Lean Thinking that is closest to the typical sensibility of SMEs because the direct presence of owners, entrepreneurs, and management in operating activities is one of the factors that distinguishes the management system of SMEs and makes them flexible. Lean Thinking, however, offers a different perspective and way of applying this logic in the sense of making it more structured and disciplined in order to avoid the distortions and inefficiencies that are typical in the Italian case (but more generally everywhere), including the excessive operational involvement of entrepreneurs and managers with the consequence of neglecting strategic thinking and decision-making processes related to innovation; the excessive centralization of decision making with the effect of preventing the development of professional and managerial skills; the excessive orientation toward the short-term and efficiency with respect to effectiveness and sustainability; and excessive improvisation with the consequence of making the processes unstable and thereby rendering improvements difficult to configure and measure.

The idea of having a management system in which managers at all levels develop and mature systematic and up-to-date understanding of what is happening in the business and the related problems and that this under-standing is not based on guesswork and abstract assumptions but infor-mation rooted in reality is the foundation of *gemba* walks. Of course, we already know that the ability to short-circuit the business decision-making process by moving down to lower levels through direct observa-tion is essential for top management to understand the reality, anticipate trends, and prevent problems or solve them as soon as possible. The Italian business world is full of stories and anecdotes of this type, from the late Michele Ferrero's swooping to the points of sale to check the freshness of Nutella, baked goods, or chocolates on the shelves to Leonardo Del Vecchio's attention to the design details of Luxottica's designer spectacle frame collections.

However, what Lean Thinking proposes is the adoption of a disciplined, systematic, and widespread application of these behaviors (and a division of labor between the management levels in implementing it) in order to always have the overall situation under control through factual data with management verifying information firsthand. In short, *gemba* walks are one of the elements of management standard work, the functional equiva-lent of standardized work that is applied by operators. Management stan-dard work is a set of routines (for example, standardized work audits using *kamishibai boards*, daily huddle meetings, KPIs board reviews, X-matrix and A3 reviews, etc.) that are strongly anchored to reality and to the effec-tive and more disciplined development of activities based on what man-agement really needs to do to add value and help others produce products and services that satisfy customers.

In Italian SMEs, *gemba* walks have a particular meaning and are an emotionally charged concept.

I am often told, "Come, I'll take you on a factory tour," skipping the pre-sentations, forsaking any preliminaries, without even needing to ask the owners, entrepreneurs, or managers of the SMEs that I visit.

For SME leaders, taking periodical, structured *gemba* walks in plants, technical departments, warehouses, offices, and call centers has become a way of grasping the business situation and understand the production context in which customers, employees, shareholders, and local com-munities see their interests satisfied and the solution to their problems materialized.

This happens not in meeting rooms, not in the offices with colorful PowerPoint presentations or spreadsheets with often illegible numbers, but in the *gemba*, where ideas are translated into artifacts, into solutions to market needs.

Gemba walks also often have symbolic meaning for SME leaders: return-ing to the essence of your work, rediscovering the meaning of what you do, watching how people and processes generate business results, and finding opportunities to reflect on these, distant from the often widespread idea that results are modifiable regardless of what happens in reality or that they are an abstraction and that their determinants are exogenous, per-haps financial or even random.

Taking a *gemba* walk also means recognizing the complexity inherent in any company that attempts to do business seriously, to daily, efficiently, competitively, and sustainably solve the problems of its customers. It means attempting to do the job increasingly better over time and real-izing that to improve requires changing the way of operating. It means not assuming anything and instead being open to surprise and the real-ity, always observing with a fresh eye and always attentive to waste and opportunities. Taking a *gemba* walk in the end means respecting one's own work and that of others, also and especially the most humble, and placing work at the center of the business and thus of the economy and society.

Italian SMEs successfully applying Lean Thinking typically adopt a management system characterized by management standard work and *gemba walks* as this allows managing the organization through direct knowledge of the issues and facts and the involvement of people.

Such a management system enables SME leaders to (a) continuously align processes and behaviors with the strategic goals, (b) stabilize pro-cesses to current standards in order to create the baseline against which to measure any continuous improvement activities, (c) focus on problem solving instead of blaming people, (d) rethink management work at all levels in a less "heroic" and more "Socratic" approach, and (e) assess how the lean transformation process is progressing and how to adjust it.

In essence, managing through *gemba* walks implies returning to basing management on facts, on reality, on the work of people, and on the application of the scientific method to solving problems to improve the business (Womack, 2011). Remaining anchored to the *gemba* is the secret of Lean Thinking and the antidote to management based on data bureaucracy, chance, on superstition or ideology because as Alexis Carrel, who won the Nobel Prize for medicine in 1912, said, "A few observations and much reasoning lead to error; many observations and a little reasoning to truth" (Carrel, 1965).

4

The Transformation Paths of Italian SMEs

4.1 THE ITALIAN WAY TO LEAN THINKING

During the last decade, the stirring and widespread attention to the application of Lean Thinking to SMEs—in Italy as well as in other European and non European countries—has become palpable.

The opportunities for interaction and learning are multiplying, the consultancy proposals are flourishing, and interesting and somewhat complex transformation experiments are spreading.

The emergence of this new consciousness should be viewed with particular favor in Italy, especially because it is also spreading to SMEs in central and southern regions and is beginning to affect local institutions and national business associations, local and regional government entities responsible for development and industrial policies, and, in some cases, even trade unions.

From this "effervescence" in the Italian industrial panorama, some important considerations can be drawn to outline possible future trajectories. The first is one of content. The Italian industrial system, also due to its fragmented and district nature, cannot expect to improve competitiveness through the application of Lean Thinking as the sum of individual improvements in competitiveness of SMEs that make up its fabric. Let me offer an example to clarify. A medium-sized company that produces furniture or kitchens in one of the famous Italian local clusters or districts can definitely start on its own lean journey and foresee reducing inventories, increasing stock turns, reducing waste, and improving quality through the just-in-time and *jidoka* tools. However, the improvements in performance that it will achieve from these interventions will be modest and laborious because the suppliers, materials, and technologies are not also working in this perspective. More precisely, this company can certainly implement the 5S and total productive maintenance

(TPM) tools for their equipment and keep it clean, reducing breakdowns, downtime and delays, and increase overall equipment effectiveness (OEE). However, it is obvious that if the suppliers of the machine tools (e.g., varnishing or polishing machines), instead of focusing on the traditional performance of their products (increasingly faster machines, ever more technological sophistication, etc.), somewhat change their strategy, focusing more consistently on ease of cleaning and maintenance of the machines themselves or on the speed of their tooling, then the investment made by the furniture company in 5S or TPM would provide a much greater return in terms of competitiveness for both manufacturers along the supply chain. Similar examples could be given for all supply relationships along complex supply chains with strong local roots (typical of the Italian case). In short, the systemic application of Lean Thinking could lead to a synergistic effect that would increase the competitiveness of the system more than the sum of the increases in the competitiveness of individual firms (Furlan, Dal Pont and Vinelli, 2011a,b).

The second consideration is one of method but reflects the aforementioned content. The actions to support companies wishing to undertake lean transformations must be coordinated at the regional, sectoral, and national levels. In particular, coordination must be based on knowledge of the most significant experiences of companies that have successfully implemented lean transformation paths. Such knowledge must be systematically and rigorously collected, made available, and shared, building intervention hypotheses and experimental projects, including territorial, regional, sectoral, and cross-sectoral industrial policies, taking into account the interdependencies among firms.

Lean Thinking teaches that only through the implementation of the experimental approach and the scientific method (PDCA) can processes be put in place that will produce the desired results in a stable way over time. It would be somewhat curious if those working in institutions and agencies wishing to support the application of Lean Thinking in businesses do not themselves apply the principles and tools first.

4.2 LEAN THINKING AND THE SPECIFICITIES OF ITALIAN SMEs

Six aspects of the Italian industrial system have worked as potential facilitators or inhibitors of SMEs' transformations. These issues might provide insights to business operators and policy makers around the world about how to undertake successful lean transformation of SMEs and how to increase the probability that small business owners undertake lean transformations and successfully lead them.

4.2.1 Small Size

Although many studies suggest that the application of the principles and techniques of Lean Thinking can significantly improve the competitiveness of SMEs (Achanga et al., 2006), and that these enterprises should have a comparative advantage with respect to larger firms in terms of flexibility and speed of adoption (Brown and Inman, 1993), empirical evidence suggests that smaller firms instead experience considerable difficulties in undertaking lean transformations (Van Landeghem and April, 2010).

Achanga et al. (2006) highlight five major inhibiting factors to the effective implementation of the principles and techniques of Lean Thinking in SMEs: (a) the lack of specific lean knowledge of entrepreneurs, (b) the lack of leadership of entrepreneurs in starting the lean transformation, (c) the lack of adequate financial resources to finalize the necessary investments to build lean infrastructures (training, specialists, etc.), (d) the lack of appropriate skills of the workforce employed, and (e) skepticism and resistance to organizational changes.

Golicic and Medland (2007) suggest that the probability of initiating and successfully conducting a lean transformation also depends on the company's supply chain and particularly their customers and suppliers. Industrial customers and suppliers already involved in lean transformation processes exercise substantial influence for two reasons. The first is related to the demands of industrial customers and suppliers and the consequent need for companies to adapt operational procedures, information, and decision making by initiating or accelerating the internal lean transformation process. The second is the fact that lean industrial customers and suppliers generally focus on the overall optimization of the supply chain and operate according to a partnership logic and the guided growth of its customers and suppliers, providing support and encouraging development, especially if characterized by the adoption of Lean Thinking.

In Italy, as in other countries, the industrial system has a dual structure with an overwhelming predominance of small and very small production units and a small amount of large or very large enterprises. SMEs have had—and will again have in the future—both advantages and disadvantages in undertaking lean transformations. The advantages are the fact that small businesses have a strong culture of hard work, are problem oriented, and tend to involve employees. Small size postulates flexibility, adaptability, and ability to change, consistent with the *kata* logic (Rother, 2009), and the high and direct operational involvement of management is in line with the *genchi genbutsu* logic. Given the flexible organizational structure, functional organizational silos do not exist, or functional boundaries are permeable. Internal value streams are short enough so that they can be mapped and improved end to end immediately evaluating the impact of such improvements on performance.

All these characteristics clearly facilitate lean transformations in SMEs.

On the other hand, small size has disadvantages. SME owners and managers lack the time and resources needed to acquire knowledge of Lean Thinking or what is required to undertake a lean transformation. Many SMEs are undercapitalized and can't afford the investment required to undertake a lean transformation. Even if they can afford it, they tend to underestimate its potential effects because of its intangible nature and its returns in the medium long run. Moreover, in most cases, small businesses' success is grounded on the insights of the entrepreneur, her creativity, and animal spirits. These characteristics, combined with management informality and the potential interferences of family politics in small family businesses, are potentially in conflict with the need to reduce variability and rigorously and systematically apply the scientific method (in the form of the PDCA cycle) to give stability to the business process and create the standard on which to base continuous improvements.

4.2.2 Agglomeration in Local Industrial Clusters

A peculiar characteristic of the Italian industrial system is the strong presence of industrial districts and larger industrial clusters (Porter, 1998). This characteristic is common to other European countries, such as Spain, as well as to many emerging countries in South America and Asia. This characteristic—that is, the fact that SMEs tend to geographically cluster in specific regions and vertically specialize by industry—is important in assessing the specificity and applicability of Lean Thinking to SMEs as well as the likelihood that lean transformation is successfully undertaken.

Indeed, if on one hand the typical spatial proximity of firms belonging to the same district is consistent with the just-in-time logic and facilitates collaboration in customer–supplier relationships and the application of pull systems, on the other hand this means that a true improvement of performance through the application of the principles of Lean Thinking is only possible as long as these are also adopted by customers and suppliers belonging to the same supply chain in the district. The cultural homogeneity that is typical of districts is a further element in favor of the dissemination of the principles and techniques of Lean Thinking as it also allows exchanging knowledge—even informally and based on social relationships—between partners and competitors in the same local area. Physical proximity further facilitates the practices of lean supply chain management and particularly intercompany collaboration, codesign, risk sharing, and joint problem solving. This can also promote benchmarking cycles and imitation among firms in the same area. However, the concentration of SMEs in industrial districts is inconsistent with other aspects of Lean Thinking. For example, the widespread adoption of the just-in-time logic could generate negative externalities for all firms belonging to the district, for instance, in the form of greater complexity and logistical congestion and higher transportation costs. Most districts are relatively closed systems, characterized by dense and stable social relationships, impermeability to innovation, and particularly to new knowledge. In these contexts, it may be difficult for Lean Thinking to take root, especially if the local labor market is closed and characterized by the absence of skills related to Lean Thinking. Likewise, the fact that the local labor market is particularly efficient and dynamic can be a disincentive for companies to invest in lean capabilities for fear that other companies, through labor market mobility, appropriate the returns of such investments.

4.2.3 Production Specialization in Low-Tech Industries

Many Italian SMEs operate in mature industries with low technological dynamism or low scientific content. There are of course exceptions (such as the biomedical industry in which some time ago Sorin and others started adopting Lean Thinking along the lines of competitors in Europe and North America), but in general, the sectors in which Italian SMEs compete are predominantly mature. In these sectors, in which productivity, efficiency, quality, flexibility, and customer service are critical success factors, Lean Thinking is a fundamental competitive weapon and an inalienable organizational capability. From this point of view, the potential applicability of Lean Thinking is virtually limitless in terms of potential efficiency and diffusion. On the other hand, the traditional inter-pretation of Lean Thinking as a set of principles and techniques designed to reduce costs and increase productivity, efficiency, and quality runs the risk of being neither appropriate nor sufficient to restore competitiveness to our businesses. The increasing difficulty in remaining competitive in terms of production costs that globalization has brought about requires advanced applications of Lean Thinking and above all in terms of product development (Ward and Sobek, 2014), in the supply chain in the extended enterprise perspective (Martichenko and Grabe, 2010; Jones and Womack, 2011), and strategy deployment in the perspective of transforming man-agement systems and the business model (Ballè and Ballè, 2005, 2011, 2014; Dennis, 2006, 2010; Jackson, 2006).

4.2.4 Strong Unions

Trade unions have always played an important role in Italy's industrial history. Thus, trade unions have and can play a critical role in the develop-ment and spread of Lean Thinking. In the past, trade unions prevalently played a restraining role, counteracting the application of Lean Thinking in large companies and especially in Fiat. During the '90s, the first imple-mentation of Lean Thinking at Fiat was severely attacked and criticized by some of the trade unions (Fiom-CGIL Metalworkers' Federation-Italian General Confederation of Labour) as "ideological vehicles" that through the associated and legitimizing regulatory conditions intended to inten-sify work and progressively demand contractual concessions to make work more flexible and therefore less expensive and more demanding (Cerruti and Rieser, 1991; Carrieri and Garibaldo, 1993). This opposition was affected by the legacy of conflictual industrial relations that did not mani-fest in other cases, such as at Electrolux Zanussi, where the experimenta-tion was less opposed by virtue of participatory industrial relations and micro-neocorporativism. In this sense, experience shows that the pres-ence of a strong ideological union has been and could be an obstacle and a factor in slowing the spread of Lean Thinking. In a completely different context characterized by the leadership of Sergio Marchionne, the Fiat-Chrysler merger, the systematic application of the world class manufac-turing system, global competition, the implementation of Lean Thinking continues today in a less adversarial manner.

With regard to SMEs, up to a certain size they are typically not union-ized. Nonetheless, local union representatives (at the province or region level) might obstruct or facilitate the undertaking of lean transformations. In my experience, when union representatives have real knowledge about Lean Thinking and have experimented and developed the relevant skills, they know how to evaluate the different possible applications of Lean Thinking and appreciate the different possible consequences on the level of employment stability and job security, occupational safety, the professional growth paths of workers, wage levels, organizational climate, well-being indicators, and worker satisfaction.

Overall, when lean transformations are not undertaken "against" workers interests and when unions are not ideologically biased, then the conditions exist to ensure that industrial relations are an enabling factor in the lean transformation process and that the managers and union representatives effectively protect and promote the interests of workers.

In this sense, an interesting case of complementary business agreements is Silca SpA, a company located in Vittorio Veneto and a subsidiary of the Swiss Kaba Group, a historical leader in Europe and worldwide in the production of keys and security devices. Silca (founded in 1770 and managed by six generations of the Bianchi family) began its lean journey in 2007—also and especially in the wake of its automotive business unit—and has gone through the recent crisis with less difficulty than others in the industry in terms of repercussions. The trade and local union representatives (mostly CISL, Italian Federation of Trade Unions) did their work, favoring the organizational change but also negotiating hard and forcing the company to confirm their industrial and employment commitments, for example, with a soft exit agreement (voluntary and incentivized) for 25 redundant employees (out of 450) and at the same time drawing up an agreement for a substantial performance bonus (1000 euro for everyone) in relation to productivity gains in perhaps the most difficult period (2012 then reconfirmed in 2013).

Assuming that Lean Thinking is always and everywhere a managerial ideology that must be prejudicially fought regardless of the actual effects on the variable interests of workers (employment, safety, professional development, organizational well-being, salary levels) is a trade union error and in some ways a "shortcut" that runs the risk of indirectly legitimizing unsustainable and unilaterally managed lean transformation paths. A prejudicially and ideologically opposed union has the inevitable consequence of delegitimizing the lean transformation process among workers, making the management task even more complicated.

On the other hand, assuming that the unions are prejudiced against any organizational experimentation activity also constitutes an error that management cannot afford to make. The suspicion at times is that this wrong management attitude could be an excuse to legitimize unsustainable and unilaterally managed lean transformation paths. Management that does not confront the unions in the name of Lean Thinking has the inevitable consequence of not only delegitimizing lean transformation among workers but ultimately runs the risk of producing efficiencies in the short term that are more than offset by a reduction in productivity, quality, and skills in the medium-to-long term that the demotivation linked to fear of layoffs, non-agreed working conditions judged or perceived as unfair, temporary employment, and low wages generates.

4.2.5 Closed Governance and Family Ownership

The majority of Italian SMEs are characterized by family ownership and the involvement of family members in management. This aspect on one hand ensures a long-term orientation, which, as described in the prevalent literature on Lean Thinking, is one of its fundamental principles (Liker, 2004). On the other hand, this entails a family business logic that could potentially conflict with the scientific method and the application of the PDCA cycle that is the basis of continuous improvement. The best situation is clearly when all members involved in the management of a family-owned and -run firm identify with the principles of Lean Thinking, know the logic and techniques, and are motivated and active in their introduction. An interesting example in this sense is Vin Service Srl, a company founded in Zanico (Bergamo) in 1976 based on draft wine.

Vin Service, with a turnover of almost 20 million euro and 70 employees, began the transformation of their production lines according to the principles of Lean Thinking in 2011, working on the cooler production line, which then became the pilot for all other lines. The same logic is being extended to other production lines through the VIMETA project. The results in terms of improved performance are very promising with significant results also for customers. The Vin Service case is emblematic of how all family members involved in management (President Riccardo Guadalupi, CEO Daniela Guadalupi Gennaro, Vice President of Manufacturing Processes Giulio Guadalupi, and Vice President of Sales and Marketing Victoria Guadalupi) have adopted the principles and the Lean Thinking logic as a shared management philosophy. As Giulio

Guadalupi symbolically states on the *Confindustria "Lean Club dei 15"* website,* "Lean manufacturing entered my life like a typhoon after a first meeting in Confindustria with Piergiuseppe Cassone. Following this, my father and sisters and I, along with Maurizio Cansone the production and lean manager, deepened our lean knowledge to then tangibly start introducing the main logic of this method of identifying waste and optimizing production efficiency. Today, the company is in the midst of a cultural revolution, propelled by the management and owners to become a company dedicated to working like the Japanese, efficiently and accurately like the Germans but with the imagination typical of Italians. This is the gist of the VIMETA project, the essence of lean manufacturing by Vin Service Srl."

A similar experience is that of the Colombini Group, founded in 1965 in San Marino and now operating with various production centers in the furniture industry also through its subsidiaries Febal and Rossana. The company has grown significantly over the last decade, combining the business succession that led Ivan and Emanuele Colombini to the helm of the company with the start of a lean transformation that enabled changing the organizational logic and management system.

Another significant case of integration between Lean Thinking and family business is FOC Ciscato, a company in Seghe di Velo (in Val d'Astico in the province of Vicenza), rooted in experience that dates back to the late 19th century when the founders were the first to harness the energy of the local Posina creek to operate a water hammer to produce agricultural tools and axes and iron rims for wagons and carriages. The company took a leap forward after World War II when Claudio and Luigi Ciscato started modernizing and expanding the production facilities and extending the range of products from the agricultural sector to construction, food, petrochemicals, heavy engineering, earth-moving, transport, and defense. Today, the company produces large forgings for the ship-building and steel industries, wind, and hydropower. Following the acquisition of De Pretto, another historic engineering company of the Turbo Man group in Vicenza, it has reached a considerable size with around 100 million total revenue and more than 400 employees. The company operates in the production-to-order world in highly competitive sectors in which technology, quality, and advanced knowledge of materials and processes are essential for survival.

---

* http://www.leanclub15.it/home/schede businesses.

This is a case in which business succession and lean transformation went synergistically hand in hand. Mario and Giuseppe Ciscato, currently heading the group, not only continued in the footsteps of Claudio and Luigi, but also seized the challenges posed by global competition through adopting Lean Thinking as reference for the business management system. To do this, as was done for the cases illustrated in the first and in this chapter, not only did they support the change but they also invested in skills and processes (from training to consulting to the establishment of a lean development office), finding in Giorgio Dorigo, currently director of operations, the person able to orchestrate the lean transformation since 2009. Worth noting is that the systematic introduction of the principles and techniques of Lean Thinking occurred at the most difficult time of the recent crisis, and precisely the efficiency results achieved through the application of techniques such as the 5S, the visual boards, and especially SMED (which allowed reducing the setup time from 200 to 60 minutes) facilitated the subsequent recovery of the market and the acquisition of De Pretto.

However, in other cases, Lean Thinking has a champion within the family (a family member who acts as promoter and facilitator of the lean transformation process).

For example, MUT Meccanica Tovo S.p.A. designs and manufactures zone valves and heat exchangers. Initially formed as a tool manufacturer, it developed over the years as a manufacturer of components for civil and industrial heat engineering (from motorized valves to heat exchangers). It is currently led by Lino Tovo, founder, owner, and chairman, and his three sons Andrea, Paolo, and Michele, members of the board of directors. Andrea is in charge of finance and control, Paolo coordinates the commercial activities, and Michele oversees technical direction and production as well as the management of human resources. Throughout its history, the company has continued to grow thanks to a series of structured expansion projects that resulted in expanding the first original plant in the '80s, the construction of a production unit specializing in the manufacture of small metal parts and the molding composite material in the '90s, a further expansion of the main plant (now around 12,000 m^2) in 2003, and opening a production unit in Slovakia. MUT currently has a turnover of €20 million and around a hundred employees. MUT started its lean transformation on the advent of the crisis in 2008. Michele acted as change agent, leading the whole family into its own lean journey. He recalls, "In the course of 2008, it was as if the rumblings were felt of what was to come.

There was a lot of talk about the crisis in the northeast and the entrepreneurial system in general. We wanted to understand more about it and assess whether it was an irreversible crisis of the system or if it was instead a metamorphosis of the latter." This intellectual curiosity was also linked to operational problems, namely, the fact that despite being a successful company that had grown while maintaining its financial strength, its ability to respond to the market remained modest. According to Paolo, "At that time, we could not comprehensively satisfy our customers. It was a paradox: We had full warehouses but customers always asked us for what we did not have in stock."

The first steps of the transformation were classic: They changed to a pull system with a supermarket of finished products and *kanban*-managed material flows. The assembly lines and mechanical processing were reorganized, switching to production cells, working intensely on the layout, equipment, machining, and assembly cycles. The work was very hard and was managed through the joint efforts of the brothers and their ability to learn and experiment, often self-taught.

The results were not long in coming, and even if the crisis made no atonement, the application of Lean Thinking led to the significant improvement of some key performance indicators. The turns of standard products went from 10 to 24, work in process was reduced by 60%, and production lead times went from 3 weeks to 3 days.

Another example is Caron A&D, a company that provides a full range of hydraulic components used in the mechanical movements of work vehicles: shaped pipes, fittings, and hoses.

Founded in 1959 by Giovanni Caron, Caron A&D started its lean transformation in 2005 when Diego Caron and his sister Andreina took over. After personally attending a training program, Diego began thinking about constructing a new lean-compliant warehouse. "I was going to build a new warehouse in 2007, but 'Super' Mario (Nardi), Pietro Fiorentini's owner, said to me, '... first apply the lean principles and see how much space and resources you can free up; only once you have done this decide whether to invest or not.' That was my good fortune, and I think I saved the company because the crisis in the autumn of 2008 caused a drop in turnover of 55%. I did not construct the warehouse but instead made full use of existing spaces, almost doubling the machine tools. The company weathered the storm and began to grow again, and above all, performance toward customers improved." Further steps were the implementation of one-piece-flow cells and of a pull system (synchronous *Kanban*) with the key clients.

These examples show that experimenting with Lean Thinking may not only be facilitated by but can also facilitate the entrepreneurial succession process. Companies such as CAREL started the succession process using Lean Thinking as a guiding philosophy. Companies such as UNOX and Frandent are educating the new generations of the family to take responsibility through the involvement of young people in the lean transformation process.

Another ownership and governance structure characteristic of SMEs in Italy as well as in other countries is that of cooperative enterprises. Also in this case, the potential for the application of Lean Thinking is very high, especially in terms of consistency between the Lean Thinking principles (involvement, workers' and customers' centricity, long-term orientation, etc.) and the values and demands of the cooperative movement. A case in point of how this potential can be translated into effective and notable results is CEFLA Dentale, a subsidiary of CEFLA (Imola) that is a forerunner in applying Lean Thinking, obtaining significant economic–financial and market results.

4.2.6 Production Variability and Semi-Craftsmanship

The strong presence of skilled and semiartisan labor typical of many Italian SMEs is both a potential problem and a great opportunity in terms of the successful undertaking of lean transformations. The reason is related to the fact that many Italian SMEs operate in the high end of the market of businesses with custom products or engineered-to-order products with small series production and high variability in volume and mix (potentially very different *takt* time) and with work content (and thus cycle times) that is very different and potentially long. Under these conditions, the adoption of Lean Thinking takes different and specific forms (Lane, 2007), and work assumes particular characteristics and is closer in content to semiartisan and knowledge work than classic repetitive line work with short cycle times.

In such contexts, the characteristics of the work to be performed and the professional legacy on which it rests are potentially at odds with work standardization and its use as a basis for continuous improvement.

I am often asked about this issue by SME owners and managers with whom I have occasion to discuss this topic. It tends to go hand in hand and is somewhat mingled with the idea that Italian workers, due to traditional and cultural traits, are less inclined toward standardization, prefer a working environment with fewer rules, and find it difficult to accept the behavioral discipline implicit in the PDCA cycle whereby standardized work is the behavioral "norm" that as a best practice is collegially applied with the participation and contribution of all through the continuous process of improving collectively and not individually. I guess this is less an "Italian trait" and more a trait common to SMEs around the world.

This issue of the work specificity of Italian SMEs intended as type of activity, type of professionalism, cultural characteristics, and behavioral orientation (in addition to trade union presence) runs the risk of being an inhibitory factor in adopting Lean Thinking to the extent that it becomes an alibi or an excuse.

The first risk is that, especially if combined with strong ideological labor relations, work standardization is seen as a bureaucratic mechanism in a coercive perspective as highlighted by Adler (1993). Under the described conditions (production variability, long *takt* time, ample tasks with high decision-making content, qualified professionals, etc.), this conception of work standardization is unlikely to result in a continuous improvement process and stops the birth of the lean transformation process.

The second risk is related to how work standardization is implemented under the aforementioned conditions and is both a substantive and a procedural risk. There is an age-old debate in the theory and practice of work standardization on how and who should proceed with standardization (using classic instruments, such as the time observation form, the process capacity form, the standard work combination sheet, the standardized work sheet, and the operator loading chart). The classic and more practiced approach (and less consistent with Lean Thinking) emphasizes the role of process engineering specialists, work metrics, and ergonomics in the standardization process and suggests that line managers (and particularly team leaders and supervisors) should have an advisory and applicative role. The approach that is more consistent with Lean Thinking dictates and the Toyota teachings is instead in some ways the opposite. Work standardization must be implemented by the workers and the team leader with the support of specialists. There are two reasons for adopting this approach in SMEs: On one side, only in this way is it possible to accumulate the specific knowledge of the process that only operators own and to determine effective and especially improvable work standards. On the other side, the involvement of operators increases the degree of perceived fairness of the standards and legitimates their autonomous application and adoption by operators.

The third risk is the replication (in different contexts) of codified solutions successfully applied elsewhere without the requisite contextualization. For example, the degree of detail of standard operating procedures (SOP) cannot but be different, depending on the specific context measured, for example, in terms of the length of cycles. Similarly, the combination of SOP, standardized work sheets, job breakdown sheets, and job instruction sheets and their joint use as visual management devices may or may not be appropriate in specific situations. It would be inappropriate to consider compensating for lack of professionalism and training of operators in the hope that the work is nevertheless undertaken according to the standards but without having secured the necessary conditions for this to happen. It would be appropriate instead if, in a context in which work standardization is mature and is the basis of continuous improvement, visual management devices facilitates standard audits and ensures continuous training by line supervisors.

In Italian SMEs, one of the most critical factors in the implementation of standardized work is finding the right balance between the emergence, compliance, and dissemination of best practices through standards and leaving operators those margins of discretion needed to interpret their role and to highlight the issues related to the application of the standards in force and improvement opportunities.

4.3 TRANSFORMATION PATHS: DETERMINANTS AND TRIGGERING FACTORS

Based on our analysis of more than 100 cases of lean transformation of Italian SMEs, it is possible to identify some "typical" paths of lean transformation, which differ according to the type of trigger that activates them. In particular, with reference to SMEs, two relevant dimensions enable classifying the adoption path: The first is the type of triggering factor, namely, endogenous or exogenous, and the second is the type of driver that activates the transformation process, namely, need or strategy. A path is endogenous if initiated independently within the company. A path is exogenous if initiated by the effect of external stimuli, exercised by external actors (customers, suppliers, banks, competitors, etc.). A path is driven by need if initiated by the company to respond to pressures on performance and in particular threats to survival. A path is driven by strategy if the company intentionally initiated it based on strategic and/or organizational (or other, for example, cultural) considerations.

Intersecting these two dimensions provides different possible types of lean transformation paths. Among the cases discussed so far, those of Pietro Fiorentini, Unox, and Carel can be classified as endogenously initiated lean transformation paths driven by strategy. Those of Caron and Frandent can be classified as exogenously initiated lean transformation paths driven by strategy. The Brovedani and Meccanica Tovo cases can be classified as exogenously initiated lean transformation paths driven by need. In this section, we illustrate some of these paths through the analysis of other cases of lean transformation.

4.3.1 The Role of Foreign Capital

One example of lean transformations of Italian SMEs exogenously driven is through the acquisitions of Italian SMEs by multinational corporations. In these cases, the "contamination" and the dissemination of the principles and techniques of Lean Thinking occurs through the full or partial acquisition of property rights, exposing and hybridizing the management and local business operations to Lean Thinking as introduced by the new shareholders or by the new ownership.

A prime example is Marelli Motori. Founded by Ercole Marelli in Milan in 1891 as a manufacturer of electromechanical devices and from 1896 fans, the company gradually developed, becoming a worldwide industry leader. More recently, in correspondence with periods of considerable difficulty, Marelli Motori—now headquartered in Arzignano (Vicenza)—produces engines for various industrial applications, and its ownership changed first to the British group Melrose Industries and recently to the Carlyle private equity fund. The interesting thing is that these changes occurred in correspondence with the spectacular transformation led by CEO Roberto Ditri. A large part of the increased value generated for shareholders during the period is the result of the considerable application of the principles and techniques of Lean Thinking.

Here, too, the advanced industrial approach of multinational ownership, combined with the energy and professionalism of local management, resulted in a combination of ingredients that enabled recovering and improving Italian industrial competitiveness.

Marbett, now part of the Rexnord Group is another example of lean transformation initiated exogenously and driven by strategy thanks to the contribution of a multinational company. Founded in 1968 by Mariani and Bettati, Marbett started its business as a subcontractor specializing in the molding of plastics for automobiles and motorbikes. A few years later, they stopped supplying third parties to specialize in the production of components for the food and beverage industry due to the high concentration of installation constructors in the region between Bologna and Parma where Marbett still has its headquarters.

In 1994, the company was acquired by the multinational group Rexnord, a group founded in 1891 in Milwaukee as the Chain Belt Company, operating globally in industrial components with applications in various fields. Rexnord has grown progressively, also through acquisitions, up to achieving revenues of more than 2 billion dollars in 2015.

In 2002, Rexnord's financial performance was respectable, and it was the market leader in various industrial component sectors. The owner, Invensys plc, a British industrial conglomerate specializing in automation and controls, ran the business with a view to optimizing cash flows and dividends.

It was at this point that the private equity Carlyle Group recognized its potential for growth and acquired it with a view to changing the structure to improve its strategy and operations. The Carlyle Group hired George Sherman, former CEO of the Danaher Corporation as chairman of Rexnord and a major shareholder. Sherman retained Rexnord's senior management and initially worked to strengthen the management team by taking on a number of qualified people with industrial experience in companies such as Danaher, Honeywell, Boeing, Whirlpool, Maytag, Timken, and Newell Rubbermaid.

Sherman and his new management team developed and implemented the Rexnord Business System, a cohesive and comprehensive set of principles and techniques inspired by Lean Thinking (and deriving from the Danaher experience) that started from strategy deployment and the voice of the customer and were applied to primary and support processes (VSM, 5S, cell manufacturing, *kanban*, pull, etc.) and the training and involvement of people. The application of this system, starting from the strategic focus and investments in certain business areas, has played a significant role in the growth and improvement in profitability and cash flows (including operational indicators, stock rotations that quintupled as a result of the new business model). Among the most brilliant operations achieved was the acquisition of the Falk Corporation from United Technologies in 2005.

The application of the Rexnord Business System enabled remaining competitive in terms of cost even in the midst of the relocation that took place until 2008.

In 2006, Carlyle sold its majority stake in another private equity firm, Apollo Management, with which Sherman and his management team had led Rexnord to a highly successful IPO in 2012, maintaining enviable levels of performance (EBITDA ratio of 20%). In 1996, two years after the acquisition of Marbett, Rexnord acquired another manufacturer, the Dutch MCC (leader in the field of modular transporters). In 2003, following major restructuring, Rexnord decided to consolidate its activities into a single European company, Rexnord FlatTop Europe, with headquarters in the Netherlands and two production plants, one in the Netherlands and one in Italy in Correggio.

The specific sectors for the application of Rexnord-Marbett technologies are mainly beverage, food, packaging in general, and the nontraditional (such as conveyor belts on the counters of sushi restaurants or to transport skiers the short distance to chairlifts).

For its industrial customers (including Krones, KHS, Sidel, and Tetrapak) Rexnord-Marbett codesigns and manufactures components and technology solutions that are then used by end users such as brewing companies (Heineken, Anheuser Busch, SAB-Miller, Carlsberg, Interbrew) and soft drink (Coca-Cola, Pepsi Bottlers, Schweppes) and mineral water manufacturers (Nestlé Waters: Perrier, San Pellegrino, Panna, San Benedetto).

Rexnord-Marbett is now 10 years into its lean transformation process adapting the Rexnord Business System to the Italian context. Thanks to Rexnord, lean production was introduced in the Correggio plant a few years ago, and covers all major business processes. In the Correggio plant, the efforts to implement RBS have been particularly focused on two aspects: problem solving and continuous improvement.

4.3.2 The Role of Industrial Customers in International Supply Chains

Unlike the frequent complaints and recriminations of many SME owners, who often see in globalization and growing competition the origin of all their problems, a number of Italian SMEs that have successfully undertaken lean transformations would not have done so had they not been forced to confront the demands of discerning customers in global and highly competitive supply chains. A first version of these paths is when customers themselves implement a lean transformation and wish to draw all the implications in terms of supply chain management by extending the same logic to their suppliers to achieve more stable and extensive improvements in overall performance. In this case, the start of the lean transformation process in Italian suppliers is imposed (i.e., the customer requests or requires the supplier to undertake the application of Lean Thinking under penalty, for example, of the loss of the business)—in which case the path is exogenously driven by need—or through voluntary adhesion by the supplier who is guided and supported in the path by the customer—in which case the path is exogenously driven by strategy. A second version of these paths is instead when the customer does not have its own lean management system that the Italian supplier adapts to but requires significant improvements in performance (in terms of quality, cost, service, innovation) and putting strong pressure on the supplier. Italian SMEs may, in this case, see the initiation of a lean transformation process as a strategic response to these competitive pressures and demands for performance improvements. Also in this case, the path is exogenously driven by need.

A good example of this path to lean transformation is Secondo Mona SpA. Founded in 1903 by Mr. Secondo Mona as a company selling and repairing bicycles and motorbikes, Secondo Mona SpA is today a major company operating in the aeronautical and aerospace industries, including defense as a supplier of onboard equipment and systems for large industrial customers, such as Alenia Aermacchi, Agusta Westland, Avio, Eurocopter, Eurofighter, Eurojet, Honeywell, Panavia, Parker Aerospace, Piaggio Aero Industries, Pilatus Aircraft, Rolls-Royce, Turkish Aerospace Industries, Zodiac, and others.

The company began operating in the aviation industry in the '20s, carrying out maintenance activities for the first aero-engines and thereafter designing and manufacturing instruments for aircraft, especially power components.

The company, which has its main factory in Somma Lombardo near the Milan-Malpensa International Airport, has grown steadily in recent years and today has around 250 employees with revenues of 37 million euro.

The company's mission is to consolidate its international leadership position as the first and second among suppliers of power systems and equipment, hydraulic equipment, and landing gear for civil and military aircraft and aerospace original equipment manufacturers (OEM).

The production plants have always been located in a rural area south of Lake Maggiore and within the regional park of the Ticino River. For this reason, the environment and its protection are always important elements and a priority for the company. In addition to observing and enforcing the obligations deriving from national and local legislation, Secondo Mona has since 2007 chosen to implement an environmental management system certified according to UNI EN ISO 14001: 2004.

Secondo Mona's lean transformation can be classified as exogenous and driven by strategy. It started in 2003 when one of its most important customers, Safran Messier-Dowty, in turn prompted by Boeing, invited its only Italian supplier to participate in a lean supply chain program conducted in Great Britain.

The exposure to Lean Thinking via customer request (a first-tier supplier to Boeing in this case) was an opportunity for the company to initiate in-depth strategic thinking and reorganization that had the primary objective of simplifying and rationalizing the value streams according to the customers. Thus, it was a radical and innovative change in approach that affected the culture and behavior of people.

The transformation began in 2003 through the direct initiative of the business owners and consisted of the launch of a series of coordinated projects and initiatives. For example, in 2010 Secondo Mona reviewed the amount and size of warehouses with the aim to reduce inventory, increase stock turns, and reduce lead times by working on the simplification of materials flows, the versatility of operators, and the wide use of visual management boards and barcode systems to manage the material flows. The significant results of this project triggered a derivative project for the overall improvement of logistics.

Another example is the design and production of a component for the B787 Dreamliner. In this case, Secondo Mona again worked with French-Canadian group Safran-Messier Dowty, a leading first-tier supplier of the Boeing group. This project, conducted in 2011, consisted of restructuring the layout of the B787 assembly areas. The area was reorganized in such a way that once emptied of articles and components of lesser strategic value (which found alternative placements) it was exclusively dedicated to assembly and verification of all parts and components of the B787 undercarriage. The project enabled minimizing the assembly throughput time all the way through testing, inspections, and quality control and packaging components for the B787. This was also accompanied in the continuous improvement process by a significant reduction in production costs (estimated at around 23% from 2009 to 2012), net of increases in materials, labor, and utility costs.

Among the additional projects that Secondo Mona has developed as part of its lean transformation are release orders and finite capacity planning, which involves reviewing the planning and control of production by updating and modifying the MRP logic previously used.

Overall, the Secondo Mona case illustrates that a position in international supply chains with demanding customers, together with the company's desire to meet the challenges and to be able to initiate significant changes, are typical facilitating factors to undertaking a lean transformation. Of course, this is an uncertain and risky path that requires substantial investments and patience in obtaining results that in this specific case began showing two years from the start of the improvement projects.

Another interesting aspect of the Secondo Mona case is that it is now, in turn, playing the role that its customer played with its own suppliers and the local context. In particular, the supply chain projects and collaboration with the lean club of Confindustria Varese and LIUC university (described in the following sections) bear witness to this role as a promoter of Lean Thinking.

4.3.3 The Role of Local Industrial Clusters

Industrial clusters or districts are not only geographical agglomerations of SMEs—as already mentioned, but also knowledge networks (Camuffo and Grandinetti, 2011). This characteristic is of particular interest to the dissemination of Lean Thinking in SMEs because specific knowledge of these principles and techniques often spreads gradually through these local networks and could, if properly governed and promoted, spread further and faster, increasing the probability that more SMEs undertake lean transformations and more of these turn successful.

Three privileged mechanisms might enable the intercompany transfer of knowledge about Lean Thinking between SMEs belonging to a district and in general.

The first is the observation of artifacts, decisions, and behaviors aimed at imitation. This mechanism refers particularly to innovations and the imitation of corresponding products and processes but also more generally to all artifacts (technologies, documents, other forms of codified knowledge) that can be usefully applied as organizational routines and are then transferable (imitable) from one business to another especially if characterized by physical proximity. In our case, the possibility for some

SMEs to observe products, processes, organizational solutions, lean tools (visual boards, layouts, etc.) decisions, and behaviors of companies located nearby that have successfully undertaken lean transformations is one of the ways through which the probability of undertaking successful lean transformations increases.

Clearly, observation aimed at imitation is more effective the more accurate it is and subject to self-reflection that constitutes a genuine process of reverse engineering of the knowledge contained in the artifacts observed and an original instance of learning by the imitating company (Szulanski and Winter, 2002). As we shall see, SMEs can effectively understand how to undertake and sustain a lean transformation by taking advantage of the various, partly spontaneous, partly designed and guided initiatives of activating observation of the production and management systems of more advanced lean companies located nearby.

The second mechanism of interfirm knowledge transfer among companies located in the same region is the density of relationships at different levels (individual, corporate, etc.) and of different types (economic and social). The most direct reference is to the vertical relationships between SMEs that are linked in the supply chain or in a broader cluster or that give rise to horizontal agreements although this second scenario is more rarely observed in traditional districts.

Indirect links also might work as potential channels for the transfer of lean knowledge even if with firms that are located outside of the district. This is the case, for example, of two companies in the same district that compete in the end market and share a supplier who has embarked on a lean transformation process or themselves launch a lean transformation process but turn to the same consulting firm or use the same training center.

Finally, the social relationships between people working in different companies should not be overlooked as cross-firm knowledge diffusion mechanisms, particularly when these do not appear to be linked to organizational relationships. It is difficult to "seal" information within enterprises when everything that has to do with production activities occupies a central position in the dialogue that take place in the district's homes and meeting places. Other indirect relationships are thus created between the businesses in the district. In this regard, as will be seen in the OZ Racing case, the diffusion of lean knowledge can also take place or at least be triggered by personal and social relationships between acquaintances, colleagues, friends, and so forth.

The third mechanism of knowledge transfer among firms located nearby is the cross-firm mobility of people. People, in our case those who have gained knowledge and experience of the specific application of the principles and techniques of Lean Thinking, can play the role of knowledge carriers in a similar way to the aforementioned artifacts. Lean knowledge that is transferred by people from one company to another can be tacit or codified and can concern different business areas, different Lean Thinking techniques, and different phases of the transformation process. This may be simple knowledge, for example, related to the use of a specific lean tool to solve a technical problem, or bundles of complex knowledge, such as managing the value stream mapping and improvement process of the entire order-to-cash cycle. An interesting example is the FOC Ciscato case briefly described earlier. In this case, Giorgio Dorigo, director of operations, played an important role as a change agent in the corporate lean transformation process. This was possible thanks to the expertise and skills gained through previous experiences in other companies that had adopted Lean Thinking, such as Blue Box, Clivet, and Speedline, where Dorigo had as *sensei* Luciano Lenotti (then general manager of Speedline but, above all, one of the pioneers of lean in Italy, having introduced lean production in SKF Industries in the early '90s).

These three mechanisms can operate jointly and therefore synergistically. For example, the probability of success of the observation–imitation of a pull-based *kanban* supermarket and milk run in supply management significantly increases if the imitator firm recruits somebody from the innovative firm that is critical for the development of the system or if the various relationships that intersect convey some useful information.

Of course, geographic proximity between district firms, beyond cognitive and cultural proximity, is a key factor in the transfer of knowledge. In particular, cultural homogeneity among companies in the district facilitates exchange due to the uniformity of language and customary relationships. However, the dissemination of Lean Thinking through interdistrict observation, imitation, or replication requires as a priority that some pioneering companies have successfully experimented lean transformation and are thus leading companies in the district able to spread the lean knowledge they gained via the described mechanisms. Two questions arise in this regard. The first, which I partly addressed in the preceding section, is where the original knowledge of the techniques and principles of Lean Thinking in SMEs that first started a lean transformation comes from. The second, which I will address in the following section, is how to make such knowledge about Lean Thinking available to other firms despite the absence of larger companies that act in this role and how to systematically facilitate and/or accelerate and ensure this process in the future.

Both questions, in fact, relate to the same issue, namely, how SMEs can ensure the capabilities necessary to undertake lean transformations. Indeed, they may seek to acquire such capabilities through the usual codification channels (from technical and scientific literature to training at specialist third-party institutions) or through the following additional methods:

1. The recruitment of human resources from outside the district who have acquired knowledge and gained specific experiences of Lean Thinking in other contexts (the case of Pietro Fiorentini explained in Chapter 1 is paradigmatic in this sense).
2. The business relationships of SMEs with raw material, technologies, and service suppliers outside of the district upstream of the supply chain and with industrial and commercial customers downstream (the Unox case in the second chapter but also the cases discussed in this chapter are paradigmatic in this sense).
3. The imitative observation of lean transformations of external competitors.
4. The participation to events, networks, fora, communities organized by certain local institutions such as banks, training institutions, or business service centers.

To be noted is that in all the above-listed methods, one or more of the fundamental mechanisms of knowledge transfer previously discussed is present, namely, the mobility of people, relationships, and observation aimed at imitation. The case presented in the next section illustrates how these can work together in triggering an effective lean transformation process.

4.3.3.1 The OZ Racing Case

Established in Rossano Veneto in 1971 by Silvano Oselladore and Pietro Zen, OZ Racing (OZ are the initials of the surnames of the founders) designs and manufactures alloy wheels for cars and motorbikes and is the world leader in both the market and the technology. Its collaborations with the most prestigious car manufacturers; its successes in the sphere of major international automotive competitions, and particularly in F1 where it is the exclusive supplier of Ferrari and Red Bull; and partnerships with the best car designers, such as Bertone, Pininfarina, AMG, Hartge, Callaway, Schnitzer, Cizeta, Strosek, and Giugiaro, have made OZ a legend in the automotive world.

Silvano Oselladore and Pietro Zen built their first craft alloy wheel in the workshop of a petrol station in Rossano Veneto. Subsequently, with the OZ wheels installed on the Mini Cooper racing in the championship rally, the small Venetian company began to become known to the public. In 1978, it became a limited liability company with the entry of Isnardo Carta, expanding by opening a new facility in San Martino di Lupari (Padua), where all production is still concentrated, and OZ thus became a global standard-bearer of the "made in Italy" value.

During the '80s and '90s, its development and internationalization were spectacular, accompanied by continuous technological and sporting competition achievements.

By 2000, the financial performance began to worsen, and the progressive deterioration of the aftermarket led the company to a profound strategic rethinking, which was later proven misguided. In fact, the huge investments to develop the original equipment manufacturer (OEM) market, with the aim of compensating for the reduction in the aftermarket, proved hazardous and generated substantial losses in part related to the lack of volume (globalization and the emergence of new markets in emerging countries shifted demand in areas not easily servable from Italy) and in part related to the gap in competitiveness, especially in the production sphere. In 2002, the situation rapidly worsened, resulting in a serious fall in sales, heavy losses, and a significant increase in net debt.

The company initially attempted to implement a traditional restructuring process, scaling the business, streamlining structures, and changing the organizational model in a market division perspective. However, already in 2004, this strategy proved ineffective because the profit margins in the OEM market were insufficient to remunerate the investments made and because although the plants in which the wheels for the different businesses and different markets were produced were the same, the business needs and management methods were completely different. Since the end of 2004, the company has progressively reduced the production of wheels for the OEM segment and concentrated all efforts on the aftermarket segment.

These efforts would probably have only slowed the inevitable decline if the company had not undertaken a thorough lean transformation process that allowed OZ Racing to survive and return to profit in over three years.

The idea of starting a lean transformation was proposed by Franco Scanagatta, a member of the board of directors of OZ and CEO of Dainese SpA. Having observed the very positive effects of the application of Lean Thinking in Pietro Fiorentini, he was first to propose that OZ follow the same path. The engineer Claudio Bernoni, now as then CEO, immediately decided to unconditionally support the application of the principles of Lean Thinking, relying on the tangible and visible results that Mario Nardi was achieving. Thus, the same American consultancy that was operating at Pietro Fiorentini was contracted, and under the leadership of John Black and Jon Sutter, the transformation process began, a process that continues today after eight years.

Since starting the lean transformation, OZ Racing has undergone profound changes at all levels: people, mentality, production and machine layouts, production management, relationships with suppliers and customers, and so forth. The *kaizen* events (more than a hundred since 2004) have played a vital role in pursuing the elimination of waste, in analyzing and improving the value streams, and generally in all continuous improvement activities. The use of the Lean Thinking tools and principles has entailed many changes. The first was a profound organizational transformation with the transition from a vertical structure by functional departments into a horizontal structure by product lines based on production technologies. The second was the use of value stream mapping and *kaizen* events to improve the value streams and reduce stock and overall lead times. The most noticeable improvements were the creation of machining lines that operated according to the flow logic (formation of one-piece-flow cells) and further significant lead time reductions through the introduction of material pull systems. The redefinition of the layout and the reduction of inventories, all changes realized through a series of *kaizen* events, allowed re-internalizing some previously externalized activities and to consolidate manufacturing operations using the freed space. The third was the downsizing of production lots and leveling production (*heijunka*) by reducing equipment and machinery setup times, particularly in fusion, a critical technological process in terms of quality that is characterized by long and complex changeovers. The fourth was a detailed rethinking of the entire supply chain and in particular the relationships with suppliers. Only in this way was OZ able to capitalize on the improvements achieved internally and achieve sustainable results over time.

A decade after the beginning of the lean transformation, the improvements in operating performance (economic and financial factors) were rather significant. Productivity increased by 50% both in technical terms and in sales per employee, lead time was reduced by 70%, and stock decreased by 200% with a significant increase in rotations. Defects were also reduced significantly.

The lean transformation of OZ Racing confirms—as illustrated by the cases presented in the previous chapters—that two critical factors of a successful transformation are the complete involvement of the top management and the need for a management team that is aligned, motivated, and competent. In the OZ Racing case, the first factor led to the situation in which the most critical *kaizen* weeks (such as that relating to the reduction of the foundry setup time) were driven in the first person by the CEO, and the second factor resulted in changing some of the key corporate figures.

However, the most important critical factor, without which OZ Racing would not even have begun the lean transformation process, was the initial contact with Pietro Fiorentini and Mario Nardi through Franco Scanagatta or, rather, the ability to "see" a functioning production and management system based on the principles of Lean Thinking. Pietro Fiorentini and OZ Racing cannot be said to be part of the same industrial district but can be said to be part of the broader Venetian engineering cluster. The three mechanisms of intercompany lean knowledge transfer described in the previous section are clearly at work in this case as in others already illustrated. The triggering factor is constituted by the relational network between companies and individuals that functions as a source of knowledge about Lean Thinking and as a potential channel to transfer it. The enabling factor is the possibility of observing other firms' practical examples of functioning lean systems that can act as a reference in undertaking or refining one's lean transformation. The supporting factor is the possibility to acquire the capabilities to undertake a lean transformation in the form of people who can play the role of *sensei*.

4.4 LEAN CLUBS, COMMUNITIES, AND CENTERS

As illustrated by the cases presented so far, Italian SMEs have often benefited from accessing resources made available by research, educational and professional associations, networks, and institutions. An example of these organizations are the so-called lean centers or lean services. In Italy, these entities are often connected and sometimes embedded in the local branches of the employer associations: they offer on-line and in person opportunities to meet, exchange information, and share experiences, and they offer training, consulting, and coaching services through cooperation agreements and/or more-or-less formal partnerships with consulting firms, training schools, or universities.

These organizations seem to be ascribable to an institutional form in the literature called knowledge intensive business services (KIBS; Muller and Zenker, 2001; Strambach, 2001) as these lean centers, lean clubs, and similar facilities offer services in terms of facilitating the transfer of knowledge related to Lean Thinking. In the majority of these cases, these are commercial services, but in some cases, SMEs, especially smaller ones, might get access to these services for free or at discounted prices leveraging on the incentives that local governments or other institutions might provide. They serve a dual function as (a) socialization structures for information exchange and transfer of knowledge between firms in a given cluster through conferences, training programs, visits, etc., and (b) structures that connect local firms with external sources of knowledge about Lean Thinking otherwise unavailable or not accessible to local small firms.

The presence of KIBS in industrial clusters in the form of lean centers together with lean clubs is a positive factor and could enable the acceleration of the dissemination of the principles and techniques of Lean Thinking by acting as a functional equivalent of companies, such as Toyota (in Japan and the United States) and Nissan (in Japan) in developing local supply networks. In particular, the activities that lean clubs carry out evoke the territorial associations of suppliers (*kyohokai*) and the working, development, and discussion groups among Toyota suppliers (*jishuken*) (Sako, 2004). Those carried out by lean centers instead more specifically evoke the development practices of Toyota suppliers and particularly the support and assistance activities carried out by Toyota's purchasing planning division (PPD) and operations management consulting division (OMCD). The former is committed to disseminating the total quality principles through the Toyota QC award, the *kaizen* management plan, and the management of suppliers association (*kyohokai*). The latter is committed to disseminating TPS through individual supplier support and the constitution of independent study groups within these (*jishuken*). Both these structures, with their counterparts in North America (the Toyota Production System Support Center [TSSC], a nonprofit organization formed by and affiliated with Toyota Motor Engineering & Manufacturing North America, Inc.) and Europe, have contributed to building Toyota's supply chain and, indirectly through managers, trainers, and consultants, many other companies in very different industries such as aerospace, retail, and health care.

In Italy, there are now many lean clubs and lean center initiatives. Some are at an embryonic stage, and others are already well established and developed. Some are very close to the KIBS archetype, and others are simply episodic initiatives or aimed at the personal interests of consulting firms. These initiatives are typically undertaken by the regional structures of employers' associations and developed in partnership with consulting firms and, in some cases, with universities and training centers. They are largely active in training, awareness-raising and dissemination activities but lacking—with some exceptions—specific and autonomous competence centers in terms of Lean Thinking. They have proliferated in recent years, often with the prevailing logic of legitimizing the local association structures and thus without a clear strategy or comparative advantage over existing experiences. Most are not highly structured initiatives (mere training courses, in many cases), and almost all are geared toward raising awareness and literacy of Lean Thinking, the development of which is mostly delegated to external consulting firms. In this way, business associations primarily play the role of professional service intermediaries also through satellite service associations.

Lean clubs are free associations of firms that interact in various ways to encourage intercompany exchanges between businesses, especially local and mostly belonging to the same region or district.

The creation of such centers in Italy is fairly recent but seems to have found growing consensus.

4.5 UNDERTAKING A LEAN TRANSFORMATION

Our research on the lean transformations of Italian SMEs suggests that any business owner, entrepreneur, or manager considering such an undertaking should make sure she understands the context and considers how its specificities might affect the probability of success of the transformation. In the Italian case, six aspects are critical: size, agglomeration in local geographical clusters, prevalent production specialization in low-tech and/or mature industries, presence of the unions, closed governance and family ownership, and production variability with semi-craftsmanship. All these are potential enablers or hindering factors of lean transformations, and Italian SMEs owners, entrepreneurs, and managers, in addition to focusing on lean tools and continuous improvement initiatives, should carefully choose how to address them and monitor them systematically during the transformation. Some of the factors are unique to the Italian context, but others are probably common to other contexts and hence of potential relevance to SMEs around the world.

Also there are some typical paths to transformation that largely depend on what the ultimate motivation to transform is. As we saw, lean transformations in Italian SMEs can be classified according to two dimensions: the first is the type of triggering factor, namely, endogenous or exogenous, and the second is the type of driver that activates the transformation process, namely, need or strategy. Intersecting these two dimensions provides different possible types of lean transformation paths. Small business owners might benefit from clarifying in which situation they are and be prepared to adjust their transformation accordingly.

Within this framework, some actors, such as potential investors (multinational companies interested in buying, first, private equity firms, etc.), suppliers, and customers along international supply chains, might represent opportunities to undertake or sustain a lean transformation. They might provide the necessary challenge and resources to get started and stay the course.

Interestingly, networks, both interpersonal and business, also might provide support in successfully undertaking lean transformations. Communities, clubs, and other local institutions active in disseminating Lean Thinking might represent useful resources especially for the smaller firms.

5

Leading Successful Lean Transformations in SMEs

5.1 ACKNOWLEDGING UNCERTAINTY

The several SMEs and SME owners and managers I came into contact with during this research on lean transformations eventually fall into one of four categories: (a) the "unaware," (b) the "thanks, but no thanks," (c) the "I did it but ...," and (d) the "transformers."

As we will see, each of these categories has variations within so that they can be articulated into subcategories. Moreover, categories c and d (and their corresponding subcategories) illustrate a characteristic of lean transformations that is often forgotten or neglected—that is, the fact that it is risky and its outcomes uncertain. SMEs falling into categories c and d show that lean transformations can have different degrees of success and even fail.

5.1.1 The Unaware

The first category that I define, the unaware, are simply those SMEs who do not know what Lean Thinking is, or, if they know, it is so far away and obscure to them that they do not care about it. Although this case is nowadays more and more rare, it might still happen that you talk to small business owners who are simply ignorant about lean. Alternatively, they might have heard about Lean Thinking but never had a chance to really learn what it is all about.

Their firms might be struggling or successful, contingent upon factors such as the industry situation, the local market, or competition or, for other reasons, luck. Among these SMEs, I am fascinated by those who are naturally well managed, especially if they are a family business. And among them, typically few, I especially like the even fewer whose management system naturally looks like a lean management system even if they have not undergone any lean treatment. Their owners and managers are my heroes as they autonomously experienced, on a different scale and in a different context, a learning process similar to the one Toyota underwent without the necessity of being exposed to all the infrastructure of lean research, training, consulting, etc., that is now so large a part of any lean transformation and of the world that revolves around Lean Thinking. Their "innocence" is what really makes them unique, and I think the fact that, in these cases, the owners and managers do not need to use the word "lean" to describe how they successfully manage allows us to go to the essence of what Lean Thinking really is. To let the reader better understand what I mean, I will offer an example (Lean Thinking applied without calling it such) drawn from one of the most acclaimed and studied companies in the world, Southwest Airlines: the famous 10-minute turn of Southwest Airlines (Gittell, 2003), which means that the time between opening the doors of an incoming flight and closing the doors of the next outbound flight takes only 10 minutes.

In this case, the lean technique referred to is single minute exchange of dies (SMED) originally developed by Shigeo Shingo in the '50s (Shingo, 1983) to effect quick die changes in the press workshops of car manufacturers and subsequently applied to a multiplicity of processes and industrial sectors, including services.

Southwest Airlines, founded in the early '70s and one of the most successful cases studied in the world for its management system, service delivery, and human resource management, now has nearly 35,000 employees, linking 70 destinations in North America, with more than 500 aircraft, and it is the sixth American airline in terms of size. Not only that, it has also always achieved profits throughout its history (with the exception of year 2001—in an industry in which losses are instead the norm) and is always at the top of customer satisfaction ratings.

Among the secrets of its success, scholars and practitioners include the punctuality of flights (which heightens customer loyalty) and very low operating costs not only due to the standardization of the fleet (the aircraft are all the same B737 model), but also and especially the ability to spend very little time (10 minutes, in fact) between opening the doors of an inbound flight and closing the doors of the next outbound flight.

The development of this operating capacity, which has become proverbial in the field of air transport, happened by chance in 1974. That year,

Southwest Airlines had bought a fourth aircraft intended to be used 50% for scheduled flights and 50% for charter flights. The Civil Aeronautics Board, however, ruled that Southwest, then a small airline, could not operate interstate charter flights. Unable to afford an aircraft that would remain unused for 50% of the time, Southwest sold it to Frontier, thereby leaving the scheduled flights on the routes the aircraft was intended for "uncovered." The problem was clear and in some ways simple: The three remaining aircraft had to ensure all scheduled flights, and to do so, they needed to fly more and remain on the ground less. How much less? Bill Franklin, vice president of ground operations, recalls that they made some calculations and estimated that the time on the ground between flights had to be about 10 minutes and, in any case, less than 25 (it should be noted that, even today, the average time of other airlines is often more than double).

The problem was solved with the commitment and contribution of pilots, flight attendants, technicians, and managers, reviewing a series of operational routines, practices, and behaviors that were consolidated and seemed unchangeable. Thus, Southwest Airlines was, for example, the first airline to test the cleaning of aircraft (waste collection) by flight attendants during the flight. This had never been done before (cleaning the aircraft took place on the ground, lengthening the time spent there) because the flight attendants (usually unionized) had very strict and restrictive job descriptions that did not cover this activity.

Although no one at Southwest Airlines was adept in the techniques and principles of Lean Thinking, nor did they know the SMED technique (in the early '70s mostly unknown outside of Japan), there is no doubt that this illustrates a significant operational improvement (quick changeovers) with dramatic effects on performance (on-time flights and available seat miles).

Southwest Airlines synchronized and anticipated the arrival time of supply trucks, conveyor belts, and luggage carts alongside the plane in such a way that they were at the gate before the plane stopped. They began cleaning, refueling, inspection and maintenance, and loading and unloading baggage in parallel (simultaneously) based on teamwork, the versatility of operators, and their "visual" coordination. The idea is that, in accordance with legislation and safety standards, as soon as the last bag is loaded onboard and the doors are closed, the aircraft starts the push-back for departure. Clearly, embarking and disembarking of passengers is another activity that affects the time spent on the ground. In this sense, the absence of pre-allocated seats and the active role of flight attendants in streamlining the boarding activity contributes to the reduction of time spent on the ground. Today, many of these practices are widespread in the field of air transport, but 40 years ago, they represented a breakthrough.

Summarizing, the "unaware" category comprises all the SMEs that might potentially benefit from Lean Thinking. With the exception of a few of them who got to lean naturally, all the others should get exposed as they are currently giving up a real option for their small business's future performance. It is obviously the responsibility of these SMEs' owners and managers to become aware; leverage all the materials, events, and other types of opportunities available to learn about Lean Thinking; and realize the possibility of undertaking a lean transformation. Besides this, however, there are two fundamental ways in which institutions can increase the probability that small business owners get exposed to Lean Thinking. The first is to teach Lean Thinking at school. The second is to have would-be entrepreneurs learn the lean startup method (Ries, 2011).

5.1.2 Thanks, but No Thanks

The second category that I define, the "thanks, but no thanks," are those SMEs whose owners and managers know what Lean Thinking is but do not give it a try. An increasing number of Italian SMEs are in this category as basic knowledge about Lean Thinking has become a commodity. Yet despite knowing, these leaders do not act. Some SME owners and managers might simply find it difficult to understand what Lean Thinking is and therefore discard it. Alternatively, they might learn about it and consider it interesting but not applicable in their case, arguing that their company is "different" (market, industry, size, etc.), and Lean Thinking is not applicable. Similarly, they might think they are doing well enough and that it is not worth experimenting with Lean Thinking and changing an organization that works. Finally, they might acknowledge that Lean Thinking might be useful but think that embarking in a lean transformation is too risky and costly. Apart from the latter case, all the others are cases in which there clearly is a knowing–doing gap at work (Pfeffer and Sutton, 2000). SMEs' leaders think they know, and maybe that is true, but this knowledge is abstract and does not turn into action. This knowing–doing gap partly derives from how Lean Thinking is presented, publicized, taught, and offered by experts (consultants, trainers, scholars, etc.)—that is, a recipe, a set of codified tools. The pride, hypocrisy, and in few cases, the arrogance of some SMEs' owners and managers also contributes to exacerbating such a gap with the outcome that opportunities to transform are actually turned down even in cases in which they might and should be seized. There is a lot that SME owners and managers can do to minimize these cases as there is plenty that lean experts, consultants, trainers, scholars, etc., can also contribute.

5.1.3 "I Did It but ..."

The third category, which I define as the "I did it but ..." are those SMEs who, having learned about Lean Thinking, experimented with it. There are two major subcategories within this group.

The first concerns those SME owners that gave Lean Thinking a try, conducting one or few little experiments, for example, with the implementation of a specific lean tool (typically 5S, alternatively, a value stream current state map, a SMED exercise, etc.). These attempts are often cautious. Leaders do not want to commit to Lean Thinking but can't resist the idea of doing something, especially if they feel the social pressure coming from peers already experimenting with Lean Thinking. They also tend to be episodic attempts, narrowly focused and typically aimed at addressing specific problems. They are not integrated at the strategic level.

Interestingly, what usually happens in these cases is that the SMEs' owners and managers say they are happy about the application of a specific tool or about the improvement initiatives they conducted (they might even go and present their case in some public event) even if everything remains unchanged (or gets worse). These experiments are only sufficient to get the flavor of some lean tool that might look fashionable or that other companies (competitors, neighbors) are applying. In some other cases, the experiments are more articulated and structured but they are not motivated by a true and genuine intention to transform the whole business. Such motivation almost always comes from the personal lean journey of the small business owner or manager.

Overall, I would define this as a "mimetic" adoption of Lean Thinking: Do something so that it seems as if Lean Thinking is adopted, but in reality, it is not. This case is frequent when some lean operations tools and practices have to be put in place to be compliant with some external requests, such as, for example, the vendor rating system of an industrial customer.

The second subcategory concerns SME owners and managers who did undertake a lean transformation but (a) are reconsidering and uncertain whether to continue or not, (b) think that the achieved results do not meet their expectations and therefore abandoned the transformation going back to status quo, or (c) recognize the transformation failed and therefore abandoned it going back to status quo. In most of these cases, the SME owners and managers seriously undertook the transformation of their business but gave up at a certain point in time because the results were late to come, the transformation was too costly or too complex to govern, resistance and conflicts blocked it, and/or enthusiasm and energy progressively disappeared. As we will see, although in some cases the transformation might not be working for reasons related to why and how it was conducted—that is, the SMEs' owners and managers did not ask or keep asking the five questions of the lean transformation framework suggested in Chapter 3—in other cases, they were not prepared to sustain the process (Bicheno and Holweg, 2008) and need to better understand the financial performance effects of a lean transformation.

5.1.4 The Transformers

The fourth category, which I define as the transformers, are those SMEs who, having learned about Lean Thinking and having experimented with it, not only have undertaken a transformation process, but are irreversibly committed to it. My best metaphor for these SMEs is that they "got the virus" and, consequently, are not going back, can't go back. They might make mistakes, suffer, and encounter all sorts of problems, but the initial choice is not questioned as Lean Thinking profoundly contaminated the organizational culture. I define this group of believers as the transformers for two reasons: first, because they have reached the stage at which the lean culture of their companies represents the key dynamic capability they count on to take on any new challenge with which they are faced and, second, because they become benchmarks and examples to be followed by their business counterparts (suppliers and customers), local peers, and community. As described in Chapter 3, they might even become transformation agents in their region or local cluster and labor market. All the cases illustrated in Chapter 1 and many other cases presented so far are examples of Italian SMEs that belong to this category.

5.2 DE-RISKING SMEs' LEAN TRANSFORMATIONS

Mr. G. is the plant manager of a medium-sized engineering company located close to Milan. He is responsible for 130 direct and indirect production staff. He is almost 60 years old; has been with the company, a family business, for 25 years; and has seen a great deal in the course of his career, which began as an operator.

A few months ago, during a visit, I had occasion to speak to him and discuss how the company's experiments with Lean Thinking were progressing.

In 2010, with the crisis at its peak, the company launched a lean program aimed at improving productivity, efficiency, quality, flexibility, and safety. The program was in line with those of the most advanced companies and was developed in conjunction with an expensive consulting firm. The intentions of the owners and managing director of the firm were excellent and were intended to aggressively recover profitability by achieving significant operational improvements in a short time, involving people and investing in them. At least this was what the PowerPoint presentation they gave me stated and was then confirmed during the *gemba* walk in the plant I did with the plant manager and the recently hired lean manager, a brilliant 40-year-old engineer, a Six Sigma black belt with significant experience abroad.

Unfortunately, things changed suddenly. In the first half of 2011, with the persistence of market difficulties, the managing director for a while considered canceling the lean program but then re-endorsed it and its related budget, convinced by the plant manager who strenuously defended it. Mr. G. and his team argued that it was a strategic program that, if carried on, would drastically improve production performance. But some important orders were canceled, and at that point, with financial performance rapidly worsening, the owners and managing director thought that the only alternative to survive was drastic restructuring. The lean program was not canceled, however, but it quickly turned into a production restructuring plan, entailing workforce reduction as well as massive operational and capital expenditure savings.

The plant Mr. G. leads had already severely suffered from the effects of the crisis started in 2008. The market downturn first caused the accumulation of unsold stock (until the end of 2008), then several revisions of production schedules (2009), then a drastic revision (2010) associated with production stoppages and redundancy payments, then longer production stoppages, downsizing, and redundancies. In September 2011, an agreement was negotiated with the trade unions providing retirement incentives and various other instruments. In fact, the staff reduction amounted to 30 people out of 130. This lowered the company's overall break-even point and reduced the costs to the extent of being able to show the banks that "what had to be done was done" and get "fresh" money.

These restructuring initiatives, however, also acted as an alibi in the sense that they had a halo effect on everything else. The drastic downsizing did not solve the company's chronic inability to explore foreign markets, to underinvest in research and development, and to effectively engage and monitor customers and intercept their needs. The result was a portfolio of mature products, a dry pipeline with no new technology to apply, great uncertainty, and dependence on a few customers themselves in crisis, demotivated commercial units all focused on managing the price lists.

Mr. G. was patiently showing me all the nice things they nonetheless were doing with the consultants: the visual boards, the value stream maps, the 5S. He explained the process that led to their creation and argued the benefits associated with the introduction of the tools. However, after a while, perhaps surprised that I seemed genuinely interested in what he told me, he could hold out no longer and said, "Look, the issue here is not the goodness of the tools, how many visual boards we put up, how many meetings before the boards we hold, whether the charts are updated on the line side, whether the supervisors respond to calls for help when the light flashes on the *andon* board. And it is not if the equipment OEE reaches the 80% target we set. The problems are others. This factory is 40 years old. We have a varied fleet. The last small investments were made in 2007. Everyone knows that we are located in a place where the labor costs are high, and everyone knows that, unless something happens, there is a probability we will not make it. But we do our work, and we can do more and better. It would be enough to create the conditions, have a clear path and communicate it properly, provide support, and give confidence to people making them work better."

I asked him what he meant by "create the conditions," and he replied, "Have the courage to choose a direction and then the patience to pursue it with determination, to communicate, to ensure that everyone understands, to listen and learn from the problems together. Instead, the owners often do the opposite. To have a free hand, they often change their minds. If the results are not obtained immediately, they become impatient and change course of action, not considering how disorienting this is, taking for granted that everyone understands and that everyone knows what to do and how to do it... Look, before the summer, we were beginning to see a small recovery, orders coming from new customers in the

Middle East. The managing director, who then had practically stopped the plant, decided to accept all these orders despite their low profitability and impossible delivery schedules. Work on Saturdays, overtime, hiring temporary staff with inadequate skills. It was a bloodbath. People no longer understand..."

The above conversation well illustrates the challenges of lean transformations in SMEs. Despite all the plans, the commitments, the investment, the support and the tools, they remain risky undertakings, in which uncertainty is the rule.

The case shows how SME owners and managers might ill design a lean transformation—segregating it to a program with little or no impact. It also shows how they might underestimate the complexity of embarking on a lean transformation as well as the necessity to adjust as conditions change but remain consistent and stay the chosen course. In addition, it exemplifies two typical mistakes that SMEs make: (a) They try to implement a set of management tools independent of the system of social relationships in the company and the quality, motivations, and expectations of the people working there, and (b) they try to implement a lean management system independent of the business mission and its strategy.

SME owners and managers have to lead lean transformations as learning and discovery processes. They need to constantly evaluate if the right things are getting done (Dennis, 2006) and assess the progress in the desired direction. There is no way to totally de-risk lean transformations upfront, no matter how much money an SME can pour into the process, the sophistication of the lean tools implemented, or the quality of the support provided by consultants. The only real insurance SME owners and managers have is to keep asking (and answering) the right questions, those included in the lean transformation framework described in Chapter 3.

5.3 WILL MY TRANSFORMATION WORK?

Before embarking on a lean transformation and also later, during the process, SME owners and managers insistently ask the question: Does lean work? They wish to be persuaded and reassured that lean will work and therefore look for implementation blueprints and comforting evidence, including cases, examples, company tours, plant visits, etc., to be convinced and make an appropriate choice about how to transform.

Indeed, if we review the scientific literature on the relationship between Lean Thinking adoption and organizational performance, we find evidence that lean works in many settings.

5.3.1 Operational Performance Improvements

First of all, a variety of studies analyzed the operational performance effects of the adoption of lean operations practices, largely concurring on their positive impact on productivity, quality, cost, service, and inventory levels and occupational safety, especially when associated with some more general, consistent infrastructure (Flynn et al., 1995; Huson and Nanda, 1995; Powell, 1995; Sakakibara et al., 1997; Claycomb et al., 1999; Samson and Terziovski, 1999; White et al., 1999; Chandler and McEvoy, 2000; Lewis, 2000; Cua et al., 2001; Kaynak, 2003; Shah and Ward, 2003; Bou and Beltran, 2005; Browning and Heath, 2009; Mackelprang and Nair, 2010; Eroglu and Hofer, 2011; Danese et al., 2012; Losonci and Demeter, 2013; Camuffo et al., 2015). In general, there is consensus on the following main positive effects on operational performance:

1. Reduction of lead times
2. Reduction of space used
3. Reduction of inventory and warehousing at all levels
4. Shorter response times to customers and deliveries (better service levels)
5. Increased production flexibility
6. Higher quality and fewer defects
7. Increased productivity and efficiency
8. Improved occupational safety

With the right support and capabilities—issues upon which we elaborate later—improving the value streams and the work through *kaizen* activities is relatively straightforward. Obviously, it postulates strong commitment, takes time, and requires consistent effort. Here, as already mentioned, SMEs have advantages and disadvantages vis-à-vis their larger counterparts. On the one hand, if they have the capabilities, they can map and improve entire key value streams—something that might be more difficult in large firms as these value streams cut across a number of organizational units—getting more sizeable operational improvements. This, together with their flexibility in making decisions and taking action, allows SMEs to be more aggressive than larger firms in attacking waste and variability. On the other hand, especially in the smaller firms, having the right support and capability might be a challenge because of resource indivisibility, investment thresholds, and difficulty in getting access to good *sensei*. Taking as a reference Koenigsaecker's (2009) $n/10$ rule, according to which sustainable transformations are characterized by a number of improvement events per year equal to the number of employees (in the targeted value stream or firm) divided by 10, it is unusual that SMEs are able to meet this benchmark, and this might be even more problematic in smaller firms and in the first year of the transformation because of the lack of capabilities and scale economies. Just to exemplify, according to the $n/10$ rule, a company with 100 employees should conduct 10 *kaizen* weeks per year. This might be unaffordable—money and time wise—especially at the beginning of the transformation and especially if capable support is not available in preparing, conducting, and following up the events.

Of the cases presented in Chapter 1, only Pietro Fiorentini or Carel, who are medium-sized businesses with fully staffed lean development offices, were able to meet and exceed the $n/10$ standard relatively soon during the transformation. And yet, as they grew and expanded, they found more and more challenging to sustain the improvement efforts. Capability development (hiring, training and developing lean specialists) was not fast enough to sustain improvement initiatives and line managers, technicians and staff had increasingly a hard time conducting them.

In addition to the commitment, determination, and energy necessary to meet or exceed the $n/10$ or other similar rules of thumb (Byrne, 2012), a key determinant of the extent and speed of operational improvement is the quantity and quality of support that SME leaders are able to provide to initiate and sustain the transformation. Clearly, less and worse support slows down and impoverishes the transformation, translating into modest operational improvements. Support implies the availability of (a) managers' time to lead the improvement initiatives and (b) lean capabilities that can be acquired and/or developed in three fundamental ways: dedicated internal people (staffing a lean development office), consulting/consultants, and training/trainers. Orchestrating these three pillars is fundamental as there are clear complementarities in investing in these three type of resources. However, who is the orchestrator is even more fundamental. In SMEs, the orchestrator typically is either a *sensei*, a seasoned consultant, trusted by the owners and managers, who leads the transformation on the basis of her experience, or (more frequent case in smaller businesses) the

SME's owner or managing director herself, provided that she has enough capabilities, developed in the field, to lead the transformation. Without an orchestrator, the transformation is likely to be aborted or fail.

Summarizing, an SME can't be transformed unless all value streams improve. These operational improvements can happen on a variety of dimensions that eventually boil down to four, described by Koenigsaecker (2009) as the Toyota True North metrics: (a) quality, (b) delivery/lead time/flow, (c) cost/productivity, and (d) human development. I would add workers' occupational safety and contend this is a sort of prerequisite goal of any transformation.

Now, although it is true that any successful lean transformation is characterized by operational improvements along these dimensions, achieving these operational improvements does not necessarily and automatically translate into financial performance improvements.

5.3.2 Financial Performance Improvements

As far as profitability is concerned, in abstract, less waste and greater productivity imply reduced costs and increased revenues, but in practice, this is true only if the SMEs can generate cash (or persuade banks and investors to provide it) and identify market opportunities to grow. In fact, operational improvements can remain only on paper if the resources they free up can't be redeployed.

For example, reducing the space used in a plant by 30% does not necessarily result in higher productivity or efficiency if the space can't be reused, if there is no money to make the necessary investment to increase production volumes, if the facility cannot be destined to another use, or if the asset or facility cannot be rented or sold. Similarly, switching to a one-piece-flow cell might allow the reduction of the number of operators necessary to operate that segment of the value stream, but this does not necessarily translate into higher productivity and lower cost if the workers, now no longer necessary in that unit, cannot be assigned to other jobs or units. Also, reducing inventories might improve net working capital and free up cash, but if the company does not reinvest it or has no plans or ideas about new products and/or markets, this will not sustain the transformation (shareholders and banks might be happy, but this is another story).

Evaluating the financial performance effects of lean is therefore a complex process, which requires not only an understanding of how the various *kaizen* activities, improving specific value streams, fit into a broader scheme eventually affecting the bottom line. It also requires systematically monitoring performance against the strategic goals and taking into account what competitors do and how markets change.

As already mentioned, *hoshin kanri* is the methodology that facilitates this exercise, supporting SMEs' strategy deployment.

Acknowledging the difficulty in linking operational and financial performance improvements, practitioners and scholars have extensively tried to estimate what might be the financial performance improvement opportunity underlying a lean transformation.

For example, based on his own consultancy experience, Ronald D. Snee of the International Academy of Quality reports that, on average, the adoption of Lean Thinking reduce total annual costs by an amount equivalent to 1%–2% of revenues in SMEs, and these results compound over the years (Snee, 2006, 2010).

Hines, Silvi, and Bartolini (2003) provide an indirect estimate of the potential effects of a lean transformation. In the sample of firms they analyze, they found that eliminable waste amounted to between 8% and 24% of total production costs, depending on the firm's activities.

George Koenigsaecker, architect of the Danaher Business System, provides an estimate of the potential performance improvements based on the 11 transformations he conducted (including Deere & Company, Rockwell International, Jake Brake, and Hon Company). He argues that a 10-year effective lean transformation typically produces a monthly productivity improvement of 1%–2% (Koenigsaecker, 2009).

Also many scholars have investigated if, to what extent, and under which conditions the adoption of lean systems leads to better and more sustainable financial performance. These studies show similar, although less consistent (Balakrishnan et al., 1996; Ahmad et al., 2004), convergence on the positive impact of lean systems on earnings and earnings per share (Huson and Nanda, 1995), profitability ratios (Claycomb et al., 1999; Mia, 2000; Kinney and Wempe, 2002; Fullerton et al., 2003; Bateman, 2005; Jayaram et al., 2008; Fullerton and Wempe, 2009; Hofer et al., 2012; Fullerton et al. 2014), firm value (Maiga and Jacobs, 2009), and stock market performance (Yang et al., 2011).

However, most of the latter studies, besides sometimes relying on perceptual measures of performance, struggle with the difficulty of clearly identifying and isolating the differential contribution of lean systems implementation to a firm's financial performance for three reasons. The first is the potential endogeneity in the relationship between perfor-mance and Lean Thinking adoption. For example, in some cases, reverse causality might be in place with successful firms being more open, will-ing, and resourceful to undertake lean transformations. The second is the difficulty in specifying counterfactuals and ruling out the possibility of alternative explanations (unobserved variables) of financial perfor-mance. The third is the difficulty of reasonably ascertaining cause–effect relationships between lean transformations (and the characteristics of the lean system in place) and financial performance. Such difficulties derive from causal ambiguity and social complexity, elements that char-acterize any process of social change. The necessity to properly analyze these aspects has been emphasized by studies in lean accounting (Maskell and Baggaley, 2003; Maskell and Kennedy, 2007; Kennedy and Widener, 2008; Stenzel, 2008), lean transformations, and lean leadership research (Emiliani, 1998, 2003, 2008; Liker, 2004; Lucey et al., 2005; Hines et al., 2011; Womack, 2011; Bhasin, 2012; Liker and Convis, 2012; Van Dun and Wilderom, 2012; Liker and Ballé, 2013; Mann, 2014), which offer a more articulated perspective of lean systems, interpreting them as sets of rou-tines for organizational learning (Emiliani et al., 2007; Koenigsaecker, 2009; Rother, 2009; Byrne, 2012), internal knowledge transfer and diffu-sion mechanisms (Liker and Meier, 2007; Liker and Hoseus, 2008; Liker and Franz, 2011; Camuffo and Secchi, 2016), and dynamic capabilities (Fujimoto, 1999; Anand et al., 2009).

The emphasis solely on profitability, however, might be misleading for SMEs. In the Italian case, although my sense is that this also applies else-where, I found almost all successful transformations focused on cash gen-eration rather than profitability. In the cases illustrated in Chapter 1, all the SME owners and managers carefully considered the implications of the transformations on the financial structure of their firms. For example, they would include in their *hoshin* the leverage ratio (debt/equity), the ratio between the companies' net financial position and EBITDA and other cash-related financial metrics, knowing that operating free cash flow is the ultimate key performance indicator (KPI) one should focus on. Some of them even reached the point of liking having bank debt covenants on these metrics as this would set the bar "high" and represent for everybody a credible commitment to the transformation.

Again, here we are not saying that SMEs' transformations should be financially driven. Rather we are suggesting that SME leaders, while focusing on operational improvements, monitor financial performance improvements as a good proxy for being on the right track and making progress on the strategic problem they set out to solve.

Summarizing, by now there is anecdotal and statistical empirical evidence that lean works, also for SMEs, and upon this evidence, an industry of lean services (consulting, training, etc.) has flourished in Italy as everywhere else in the world.

But this evidence and the fact that it is possible to specify, at least to some extent, under which conditions this happens, does not guarantee that a lean transformation will be successful.

It is important for SME owners and managers to recognize that extant research clearly shows there is variation in the outcomes. Some firms significantly benefit from the adoption of lean thinking, others don't. In order to reduce such variation in the performance effects of lean transformations as well as the associated risk, two things eventually matter: (a) properly understanding and designing the transformation process before getting started and (b) continuously monitoring and reassessing the transformation process as it unfolds and technologies and markets change.

We believe that SME owners and managers might mitigate the risk of failing if they use the five questions of the lean transformation framework depicted in Chapter 3. The lean transformation framework will not eliminate uncertainty, but it will help SMEs owners and managers to model and cope with it.

5.4 UNDERSTANDING FINANCIAL PERFORMANCE DYNAMICS DURING TRANSFORMATIONS

In order to further convince SME owners and managers that lean transformations work and that there is variation in the outcomes of lean transformations and to provide a more accurate picture about what to expect in terms of financial performance during the transformation itself, the results of a recent study on a sample of 100 Italian industrial SMEs that seriously undertook a lean transformation might be helpful.

These 100 SMEs were selected as follows: We asked the local branches of the Italian employers association (Confindustria) to nominate a set of SMEs (defined as firms with less than €0.5 billion revenues) that were known as firms that had seriously undertaken lean transformations. We gathered 145 nominations that we cross-checked using (a) our knowledge of the Italian lean movement, (b) the results of analysis of secondary sources (press, magazines, web, firms' financial reports), and (c) a panel of consulting firms (Porsche Consulting, JMAC, Kaizen Institute, McKinsey, Galgano, Praxi, Auxiell). We used multiple sources to get confirmation about the seriousness of the transformation undertaken and avoid the risk of including in the sample inappropriate companies.

We ended up with a sample of 100 SMEs at different stages of the lean transformation process, belonging to diverse industrial sectors and having different sizes and types of ownership.

Table 5.1 list the 100 SMEs included in the sample, indicating the year of start of their lean transformation.

In order to evaluate the effects of lean transformations on the financial performance of this sample of SMEs, we focused on two financial metrics often used in the literature and in practice as they are tightly linked to the adoption of Lean Thinking (Maskell and Baggaley, 2003): (a) the earnings before interest, taxes, depreciation, and amortization (EBITDA) margin, which is a measure of the firm's profitability and is a proxy for the cash flow generated per dollar unit of sales, and (b) the return on invested capital (ROIC) ratio, which is a profitability measure that takes into account the capital, the firm's cash flow generation and its operating and structural efficiency. We measured them as follows:

$$\text{EBITDA Margin} = \text{EBITDA/Sales Revenue (\%)}$$

$$\text{ROIC} = \text{NOPAT}^*/\text{Net Invested Capital}^\dagger \text{ (\%)}$$

In order to assess the differential effect of undertaking a lean transformation, our research needed to be able to perform meaningful cross-firm comparisons, do this across industries (characterized by structurally different trends and absolute levels of profitability), and do this longitudinally. In fact, we not only want to know if the financial performance of a SME undergoing a lean transformation improves, but we want to understand if and how that happens over time and if there is any difference with how the industry and its non-lean peers do.

---

[*] Net operating profit after taxes (NOPAT) = EBIT*(1 − *t*), where EBIT = earning before interests and taxes; and *t* = corporate tax. It is a measure of operating efficiency and a proxy of the potential cash earnings of the company.

[†] Net invested capital (NIC) = net debt position + equity, where net debt position (NDP) = financial liabilities − cash and cash equivalents.

TABLE 5.1

Sample of Lean Italian SMEs

Company Name	Year of Start of Lean Transformation	Location in Italy	ATECO (NACE-SIC) Industry Code
Acque Vicentine	2009	Veneto	36
Air Liquide	2010	Veneto	28
Alfa Laval	2005	Lombardia	28
Anodica Trevigiana	2007	Veneto	25
Aprilia Racing	2005	Toscana	45
Ares Line	2011	Veneto	31
Argomm	2006	Lombardia	22
Artemide	2007	Lombardia	27
Ase	2009	Lombardia	26
AskollDue	2006	Veneto	32
Baltur	2007	Emilia Romagna	28
Baxi	2005	Veneto	27
Berto's	2010	Veneto	27
Blue Box Group	2008	Veneto	28
Bortolin Kemo	2008	Friuli Venezia G.	28
Brevi	2008	Lombardia	32
Brovedani	2008	Friuli Venezia G.	25
Bticino	2001	Lombardia	27
Bucher Hydraulics	2001	Emilia Romagna	28
Caron	2006	Veneto	24
Cielo e Terra	2010	Veneto	11
Climaveneta	2004	Veneto	28
Clivet	2007	Veneto	28
CMS	2006	Emilia Romagna	25
Cofibox	2006	Lombardia	22
Cordivari	2005	Abruzzo	25
Danfoss	2008	Emilia Romagna	28
De Iuliis Macchine	2005	Campania	28
Emilceramica	2008	Emilia Romagna	23
Eurosets	2011	Emilia Romagna	32
Eurotermo	2007	Lombardia	28
Falegnami Italia	2005	Toscana	31
Farid Industrie	2006	Piemonte	45
Fava	2004	Emilia Romagna	28
Foc Ciscato	2010	Veneto	25
Frandent	2009	Piemonte	28

(Continued)

TABLE 5.1 (CONTINUED)

Sample of Lean Italian SMEs

Company Name	Year of Start of Lean Transformation	Location in Italy	ATECO (NACE-SIC) Industry Code
Friuli Intagli	2011	Friuli Venezia G.	31
Giletta	2005	Piemonte	28
Glem Gas	2005	Emilia Romagna	27
GSG International	2007	Emilia Romagna	25
Harken	2007	Lombardia	30
Hydroven	2011	Veneto	28
Ilcam	2005	Friuli Venezia G.	31
IML Motori	2009	Lombardia	25
IMS Deltamatic	2008	Lombardia	28
Inglesina	2008	Veneto	30
Inipress	2008	Veneto	22
Inox Laghi	2008	Lombardia	46
Inver	2009	Emilia Romagna	20
Karton	2006	Friuli Venezia G.	22
Keyline	2011	Veneto	25
Lafert	2006	Veneto	27
Lago	2006	Veneto	31
Laverda	2011	Veneto	28
Lowara	2003	Veneto	28
Lucaprint	2008	Veneto	17
Manitowoc	2006	Piemonte	28
Maschio Gaspardo	2008	Veneto	28
Meccanostampi	2011	Veneto	25
Meccanotecnica Umbra	2009	Umbria	25
Micro Detectors	2011	Emilia Romagna	33
Midac	2007	Veneto	27
Minifaber	2010	Lombardia	25
Mipharm	2004	Lombardia	21
Mollebalestra	2009	Piemonte	25
Moog Italiana	2009	Lombardia	46
MUT Meccanica Tovo	2008	Veneto	28
Navalimpianti	2009	Liguria	30

(Continued)

TABLE 5.1 (CONTINUED)

Sample of Lean Italian SMEs

Company Name	Year of Start of Lean Transformation	Location in Italy	ATECO (NACE-SIC) Industry Code
Nobili	2011	Emilia Romagna	28
Omet	2009	Lombardia	28
OMP Porro	2009	Lombardia	25
Paradisi	2009	Marche	25
Pietro Fiorentini	2000	Veneto	28
Pilot	2009	Lombardia	17
Pomini	2009	Lombardia	28
Praxair	2006	Lombardia	25
Presotto Industrie Mobili	2010	Friuli Venezia G.	31
RDS Moulding	2008	Veneto	24
Rexnord	2004	Emilia Romagna	22
Robur	2006	Lombardia	28
Roncadin	2011	Friuli Venezia G.	10
Schaeffler	2009	Piemonte	28
Seco	2009	Lombardia	25
Secondo Mona	2003	Lombardia	28
Sicon	2005	Veneto	26
Silca	2007	Veneto	25
Sisma	2010	Veneto	28
Slimpa	2008	Lombardia	28
Speedline	2009	Veneto	24
Stanadyne	2006	Lombardia	25
Tecnoform	2010	Emilia Romagna	31
Tecnomatic	2010	Lombardia	28
Tellure Rota	2006	Emilia Romagna	25
Thermowatt	2010	Marche	25
Valmex	2011	Marche	28
Vertex Pistons	2009	Emilia Romagna	30
Videotec	2009	Veneto	26
Vimi Fasteners	2010	Lombardia	25
Vin Service	2009	Lombardia	28
Watts Industries	2009	Trentino Alto A.	28

Therefore, we started by normalizing the sample lean SMEs' financial performance. More specifically, we analyzed if each firm in our sample over- or under-performed a set of non-lean competitors regarding the above profitability measures. In order to do this, first we transformed each dependent variable into an index number, which highlighted the differential performance of each company compared with a group of industry peers that did *not* undertake a lean transformation;

$$D_{v,f,t} = \frac{X_{v,f,t} - m_{v,f,t}}{|m_{v,f,t}|} + 1$$

where

$D_{v,f,t}$ = industry normalized performance variable (EBITDA ratio and ROIC) – index number

$X_{v,f,t}$ = value of performance variable v in the firm f in the year t

$m_{v,f,t}$ = industry median value of performance variable v in the firm f in the year t

The underlying assumption is that, after controlling for industry-specific factors and choosing peer groups appropriately (competitors that did *not* undertake a lean transformation), the differential performance of the analyzed firms should be reasonably attributed to their lean transformation. Again, the non-lean competitors' median financial performance level was determined using the coarsened exact matching procedure (Blackwell et al., 2009), i.e., by identifying, for each lean firm in the sample, a panel of industry peers or competitors *not* undergoing a lean transformation. Peer groups comprised 10 to 20 non-lean competitors that were selected according to the following criteria: (a) same SIC-NACE (national industry classification category) code of the lean SME included in the sample, (b) Italian SMEs, and (c) closest size-wise to the analyzed lean SMEs.

Once the financial performance data of each lean SME in the sample was industry normalized (against non-lean competitors), we calculated—for each of the analyzed firms and for each of the performance variables (EBITDA ratio and ROIC transformed into an index number as described above)—the performance variations over time since the start date of the lean transformation. We calculated the industry (non-lean competitors) normalized financial performance percentage increase/decrease that occurred from *before* the implementation of lean production systems to 2015. To avoid distortions due to particular events occurring right before the start of the implementation, we considered the average of the industry normalized financial performance measures of the three years before the lean transformation as the baseline performance.

Lean transformation performance up to 2015:

$$LJ_{v,f,2011} = \frac{D_{v,f,2011} - D_{v,f,initial}}{\left| D_{v,f,initial} \right|}$$

where

$D_{v,f,2011}$ = value of the industry normalized performance variable v in the firm f in the year 2015

$$D_{v,f,initial} = \frac{D_{v,f,t_0} - D_{v,f,t_0-1} + D_{v,f,t_0-2}}{3}$$

t_0 = year of start of lean system implementation

This indicator allows the appreciation of the overall performance change by each firm from the start of implementation to 2015 relative to their non-lean competitors.

Figures 5.1 and 5.2 report the median percentage variation of the industry normalized EBITDA margins and ROIC ratio for the sample of 100 lean Italian SMEs. They show by how much the lean sample has under- or over-performed its non-lean competitors in terms of performance change after one, two, three, four, five, six, and seven years since the start of the lean transformation (after seven years, sample size becomes to small not allowing for meaningful analysis).

Taking the years before the beginning of the lean transformation as the baseline (it corresponds to zero), the graphs show by how much the lean sample improved or worsened vis-à-vis its competitors. Observations in the negative range represent years in which the lean sample improved less than its competitors. Observations in the positive range correspond to years in which the lean sampled improved more than its competitors.

Interestingly, the lean transformations of the analyzed sample of lean Italian SMEs seem to generate nonlinear performance effects over time. Initially, performance worsens, with non-lean SMEs doing better in the first year of the lean SMEs' transformations. However, after the second year from the beginning of the transformation, lean SMEs tend to outperform

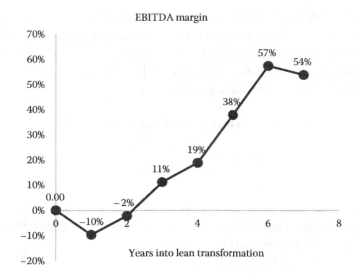

FIGURE 5.1
Lean Italian SMEs' median—industry normalized—EBITDA margin variation during lean transformation. $N = 100$. Results from author's analysis on ORBIS–Bureau Van Dijk financial statements' data.

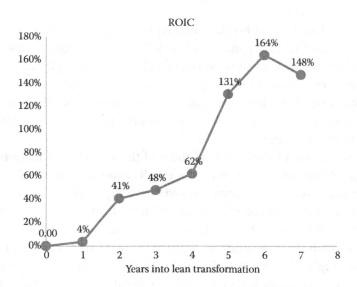

FIGURE 5.2
Lean Italian SMEs' median—industry normalized—ROIC variation during lean transformation. $N = 100$. Results from author's analysis on ORBIS–Bureau Van Dijk financial statements' data.

their non-lean competitors with spectacular performance differentials five years into the transformation.

Table 5.2 reports the sample composition/size and average, median, and standard deviation of the performance variation of the analyzed lean Italian SMEs after one, two, three, four, five, six, and seven years from the beginning of the lean transformation.

The performance variation distributions are very skewed with big variations and outliers.

Focusing on sample medians as the more informative descriptive statistic, we observe that in the first year of lean transformation lean SMEs tend to do no better than their competitors (they even get comparatively worse in terms of EBITDA margin). After the second year, however, lean SMEs' performance changes (normalized compared to those of their competitors) are significantly higher. EBITDA margin improvements go from 11% after three years to more than 50% after seven years. ROIC progression is even steeper moving from 4% in year one of the lean transformation to 1.5 times after seven years.*

The data are consistent with extant lean accounting literature, which suggests that there is a time lag between the adoption of lean systems and financial performance improvements. Two main factors explain this lag (Maskell and Baggaley, 2003; Maskell and Kennedy, 2007; Stenzel, 2008). The first is operational and is linked to the negative effects that, at first, the implementation of lean operations practices might have on business processes. Plant layout changes; redefinition of work standards; changes in the logic of production planning and control; and intensive training of workers, technicians, and management (all brought about by the start of the lean transformation), among others, cause significant operational disruption and deterioration of performance in the short term. Only after completing the initial transition to lean practices does financial performance start to improve as the effect of operational performance improvements also kicks in.

The second is financial in nature and refers to accounting effects. In fact, apart from the problems of traditional cost accounting systems, the first main result of starting a lean transformation is typically waste

---

* We also conducted further statistical analyses testing the alternative hypothesis of abnormal profitability for the SMEs included in the lean sample vis-à-vis three samples of non-lean firms randomly drawn from the comparables used in the analysis (non-lean competitors, same SIC-NACE industry code, approximately same size). The non-parametric statistical analysis results (Mann–Whitney U test) suggest that we reject the hypothesis for the first and second year of transformation and accept it from year three on. This basically confirms that making investments in a portfolio of SMEs credibly committed to a lean transformation would typically be more remunerating than investing in a portfolio of similar non-lean SMEs.

TABLE 5.2

Sample Composition/Size and Average, Median, and Standard Deviation of the Performance Variation of the Analyzed Lean Italian SMEs after One, Two, Three, Four, Five, Six, and Seven Years from the Beginning of the Lean Transformation

Lean Transformation	# Firms	EBITDA/Revenues			ROIC		
		Mean	Median	Standard Deviation	Mean	Median	Standard Deviation
Time 0	100	0.00	0.00	0.00	0.00	0.00	0.00
1 year	100	1%	−10%	261%	900%	4%	8624%
2 years	100	43%	−2%	283%	925%	41%	5846%
3 years	100	−759%	11%	7860%	1040%	48%	6049%
4 years	89	109%	19%	392%	1583%	62%	9205%
5 years	78	127%	38%	368%	1705%	131%	7615%
6 years	60	284%	57%	1559%	1942%	164%	7090%
7 years	43	726%	54%	4031%	2113%	148%	8574%

elimination and variability reduction. These often take the form of stopping overproduction, reduction of inventories, and, more generally, the freeing up of resources (in the form of space, capacity, people, time, skills, etc.). In the abstract, these resources are redeployable for other uses or can be made otherwise available. In practice, this does not happen—at least immediately—for reasons related to resource stickiness, technological constraints, and institutional rigidities. Therefore, unless and/or until complementary choices about the use of these resources are made by the SMEs' owners and managers, the waste elimination does not translate into financial performance improvements (relative to non-lean competitors). This is a key reason why it is important ask the five questions of the lean transformation framework described in Chapter 3 and, more specifically, the first one: What is the strategic problem we are trying to solve? Furthermore, this is a key reason why *hoshin kanri* or strategy deployment is, among all the lean tools, probably the most important as it allows the consistent and effective identification of how the freed up resources can be used for development strategies or to reduce excess capacity and slack.

In both cases, on the one hand, the impact of *kaizen* activities on the income statement and the balance sheet is not immediate but becomes visible later with time-lagged financial indicators. On the other hand, the effects of *kaizen* activities on the income statement differ contingent on the strategic decisions referred to above, possibly leading to improvements in profitability either through revenue increases thanks to development activities (first case) or mainly via cost (opex and/or labor) reductions through downsizing (second case).

Moreover, as lean transformations initially often focus on waste elimination through inventory reduction and destocking, inventory write-downs might also affect the income statement. Similarly, avoiding overproduction might imply that some of the indirect or general costs typically attributed to products through standard full costing techniques will no longer translate to the balance sheet as inventories (assets). Instead, a portion of these costs might surface and negatively impact the profit and loss statement.

These factors contribute to generating the apparent null effect (or even comparative worsening of the financial performance) that often characterizes the early stages of lean transformations and that is confirmed by our analysis of Italian SMEs.

SME owners and managers should be aware of these effects as the operational disruption and initial stickiness or deterioration in financial performance might have a discouraging effect and persuade them to discontinue lean efforts and/or abandon the transformation.

However, typically three years after the beginning of the transformation, SMEs sustaining their transformation dramatically outperform their non-lean industry peers.

However, SME owners and managers should not be misled by the sample medians and averages. If they wish to fully appreciate what to expect during a lean transformation, they should pay much attention to the distribution (not only the median) of the industry normalized performance variations. For example, the standard deviations reported in Table 5.2, as well as the ranges reported in Figures 5.3 and 5.4, confirm that some firms significantly benefit from the undertaking of a lean transformation, and others don't. Some lean SMEs do better than their non-lean counterparts and vice versa.

It is therefore extremely important that SME owners and managers, rather than focusing their attention on lean tools, spend as much time as possible making sure that such potential variation in the outcomes of their lean transformation is reduced. Again, the five questions of the lean transformation framework described in Chapter 3 represent a powerful countermeasure to design and de-risk the transformation process.

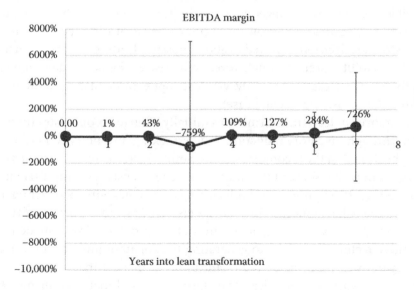

FIGURE 5.3

Lean Italian SMEs' average and deviation—industry normalized—EBITDA margin variation during lean transformation. $N = 100$. Results from author's analysis on ORBIS–Bureau Van Dijk financial statements' data.

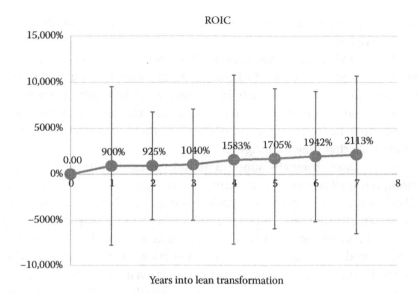

FIGURE 5.4
Lean Italian SMEs' average and deviation—industry normalized—ROIC variation during lean transformation. $N = 100$. Results from author's analysis on ORBIS–Bureau Van Dijk financial statements' data.

Overall, this study underlines that SMEs' leaders wishing to undertake a lean transformation need to (a) make a serious and lasting commitment to transform, avoiding the temptation, as in the case described in Section 5.2, to change course of action and/or abandon it; (b) choose accurately the value streams that require more urgent improvement as defined by strategy deployment; (c) build enough capabilities and create an adequate lean infrastructure to sustain the transformation; and (d) embrace Lean Thinking completely, leading by example by going to *gemba* to see and creating a culture that goes beyond the visible devices and artifacts of lean tools.

5.5 MAKING IT WORK

There is no way to know upfront if a lean transformation will work and lead to achieving the desired results. Unfortunately, this uncertainty runs the risk of either blocking the undertaking of lean transformations by SMEs' owners and managers or making them question their commitment, discouraging them, and possibly making them abandon the process of transformation.

At times, this uncertainty entails a kind of hasty anxiety, often more common among those new to Lean Thinking, who after an initial smattering of lean tools would like to immediately obtain results, instantly see the impact on operations or even in the income statement and cash flows, almost more to legitimize their position or their own decisions and to demonstrate that they were right.

In other cases, it entails substantial and perhaps undisguised concern among those who lead and/or champion the lean cause and act as "evangelists" in the company transformation. It might be that results are slow in coming. Quality does not improve. Productivity—as measured for example by overall equipment effectiveness (OEE) is at a standstill. Even costs do not seem to decrease after some initial reduction. "Why aren't we making progress?" This is a legitimate question that is even more pressing in light of certain unrestrained journalistic and consultancy rhetoric chanting about +x% more productivity, –y% stock, +z% quality, and so forth (where x, y, and z are, of course, double-digit figures over monthly time horizons).

I think it is important to critically address the issue of lean transformation outcomes by clarifying some basic misunderstandings and providing some practical suggestions on how to obtain the desired results from lean transformations.

As we saw in the previous section, it is not easy to evaluate the overall impact of a lean transformation on a firm performance calculating the associated return on investment.

One possibility is to apply the discounted cash flow method (DCF) to calculate the net present value of the investment in a lean transformation.

This exercise can be done retrospectively, for analytic purposes, or upfront to make decisions (following a capital budgeting approach, which is extremely complex to do in this case). We conducted a retrospective exercise in some of the Italian SMEs included in the above-described sample. For example, at Pietro Fiorentini, we asked the finance department to provide detailed data on all the expenditures (operational and capital) related to the lean transformation, by year, since 2000 (start of the lean transformation). Then, we estimated the increased revenues and cost savings, by year, attributable to the lean transformation. This was the most difficult part of the exercise as a number of endogenous and exogenous variables affect revenue and cost dynamics together with *kaizen* activities. Pietro Fiorentini's *hoshin kanri* and A3 portfolio was used to make better-informed estimates on this matter. On the basis of these estimates of lean transformation–related cash inflows and outflows by year, and using Pietro Fiorentini's cost of capital as discount rate, we ended up with the net present value of the investment in lean transformation. The results of these exercises, which we cannot disclose for confidentiality reasons, are extremely informative about the potential of lean transformations in SMEs. A similar, more complex evaluation exercise was conducted, on the same data, modeling lean as a real option (Trigeorgis, 1995; Kogut and Kulatilaka, 2001).

All these provisional and retrospective analyses should be geared toward reducing the gaps SMEs often experience between the actual and potential benefits that lean can generate from a financial standpoint as well as the gaps between the operational and the financial improvements. As we saw in Chapter 3, these gaps might be due to insufficient management commitment to the transformation and inadequate investment in capabilities (amount and quality of support). As regards this latter point, although it is impossible to provide general benchmarks, our sense is that successful lean Italian SMEs do create teams of lean specialists (lean development office, *kaizen* promotion office, etc.). Smaller firms (up to 100 employees) prevalently count on external support via consultants and have their key people (the owner, the family members, etc.) spending considerable amounts of time in the transformation. Larger firms tend to acquire and develop internal expertise (with staffing ratio for the lean development offices up to 3% of the workforce—full time equivalent). In many cases, the critical issue is the quality of this support. Smaller firms have more difficulty in accessing good *sensei* and effective consultants. Consequently, the quality and speed of improvement is often comparatively lower.

When these issues have been resolved, successful transformations of Italian SMEs suggest that there are four ways to increase the likelihood that lean transformation efforts translate into financial results.

The first is the choice of markets, products, or value streams on which to focus the lean transformation. Lean has to be applied to a sufficiently ample market, product, or value stream combination where there is potential for significant improvement because the waste in current practices is very high and because increased efficiency frees up resources to grow the business. The second is the choice of where to focus investments and decide to improve through lean once the market, product, or value stream on which to act has been selected. A basic principle of *kaizen* is to focus improvement activities based on the needs and priorities arising from critical strategic and operational elements (e.g., through *hoshin kanri*), namely, based on KPIs that capture the strategic problem the company is trying to solve. It would be wrong instead to proceed with improvement activities based simply on what is immediately visible and/or easily practicable. Improving is always possible, but knowing where to place the betting chips (usually a few) with reasonable certainty that they will produce results is a key organizational capacity. In many plants I visit, I see a lot of improvement activities in progress and many ongoing projects. However, how these activities interact with each other and the causal relationship between these and the financial performance is a matter that needs to be addressed through *hoshin kanri*.

The third is to multiply the operational improvements by spreading them between organizational units, business units, and possibly companies (*yokoten*). Getting this multiplicative effect is not easy and requires discipline and organizational routines that SMEs often do not have. Also, many lean development officers tend to stop at the point *kaizen* is attained in a specific process and consider this improvement as a point of arrival rather than as a point of departure for diffusion.

The fourth is to remember that the extent of the change of the financial performance can only be proportional to the extent of the change of the operational performance, which is proportional to the extent of the change in processes and people. Processes and people that remain (almost) unchanged are unlikely to produce much better results.

5.6 CRAFT YOUR OWN TRANSFORMATION AVENUE

SME owners and managers have a great opportunity: Undertake or sustain lean transformations to create wealth and jobs. Lean transformations' outcomes are uncertain, and the main role of the SMEs' leaders is to de-risk them as much as possible. Uncertainty cannot be eliminated, but can be effectively modeled. One useful way of doing this is to use the lean transformation framework illustrated in Chapter 3. This framework proposes a situational approach to lean transformations and consists of asking, before and during the transformation, five questions related to the strategic problem to solve, the value streams that need to be improved, the capabilities that have to be acquired and developed, the management system and leadership required, and the basic thinking on which the organizational culture is rooted. Answering coherently these five questions allows, over time, leading the transformation effectively. Interestingly (and differently from conventional wisdom) the lean transformation framework not only suggests that lean systems will differ over time and across firms as the learning/discovery process underlying the transformation unfolds, but also that there are multiple paths to transformation (Camuffo and Gerli, 2016). For example, a small company whose survival is at risk will probably focus on cash flows, cost, and efficiency and will invest the few resources available for everything in trying to improve the value streams, emphasizing the necessary tools, and leveraging external capabilities to get quick results. The leaders will also focus on operational improvements, transmitting a sense of urgency, and the need to make quick progress. These will reflect on the characteristics of the management system and on leadership behaviors. A small company that, instead, is doing well and targets growth or an innovative business model can emphasize more capability building and make sure that the *kaizen* activities not only improve the processes, but also change the culture. In this case, the leaders can spend more time coaching and teaching as well as involving all the employees in the transformation process. In any case, SME leaders need to avoid the widespread approach, which assumes that implementation takes place linearly, cascading a predefined, codified set of lean practices and following a predetermined sequence of steps, including communication about the intention to implement a lean system, the appointment of a team of lean specialists supported by external consultants to steer the process, people training about lean operations practices, etc.

SME leaders must find their own way. It will be a lot of work and a lot of fun.

Bibliography

Accornero, A. (2009). Work and class: FIOM's great survey. *Lavoro e diritto, 23*(3), 337–350.

Achanga, P. et al. (2006). Critical success factors for lean implementation within SMEs. *Journal of Manufacturing Technology Management, 17*(4), 460–471.

Adler, P. S. (1993). Time and motion regained. *Harvard Business Review*, January–February, 97–108.

Ahmad, A., Satish, M., & Pletcher, M. (2004). The perceived impact of JIT implementation of firms' financial/growth performance. *Journal of Manufacturing Technology Management, 15*(2), 118–130.

Ahmad, A., Schroeder, R. G., & Sinha, K. K. (2003). The role of infrastructure practices in the effectiveness of JIT practices: Implications for plant competitiveness. *Journal of Engineering and Technology Management, 20*, 161–191.

Akao, Y. (ed.) (2004). *Hoshin Kanri: Policy Deployment for Successful TQM*, Productivity Press, New York.

Allen, C. R. (1919). *The Instructor, The Man and The Job*, Lippincott Company.

Anand, G., Ward, P., Tatikonda, M., & Schilling, D. (2009). Dynamic capabilities through continuous improvement infrastructure. *Journal of Operations Management, 27*(6), 444–461.

Balakrishnan, R., Linsmeier, T. J., & Venkatachalam, M. (1996). Financial benefits from JIT adoption: Effects of customer concentration and cost structure. *The Accounting Review, 71*(2), 183–205.

Ballé, F., & Ballé, M. (2005). *The Gold Mine: A Novel of Lean Turnaround*. Lean Enterprise Institute, Cambridge, MA.

Ballé, F., & Ballé, M. (2011). *The Lean Manager*. Lean Enterprise Institute, Cambridge, MA.

Ballé, M., & Ballé, F. (2014). *Lead with Respect: A Novel of Lean Practice*. Lean Enterprise Institute, Cambridge, MA.

Banerjee, A. V., & Duflo, E. (2011). *Poor Economics: A Radical Rethinking of the Way to Fight Global Poverty*, Public Affairs, USA.

Bateman, N. (2005). Sustainability: The elusive element of process improvement. *International Journal of Operations & Production Management, 25*(3), 261–276.

Bell, S. C., & Orzen, M. A. (2010). *Lean IT: Enabling and Sustaining Your Lean Transformation*. CRC Press, New York.

Bhasin, S. (2012). An appropriate change strategy for lean success. *Management Decision, 50*(3), 439–458.

Bicheno, J., & Holweg, M. (2008). *The Lean Toolbox. The Essential Guide to Lean Transformation*. PICSIE Books, Buckingham.

Black, J. (2007). Design rules for implementing the Toyota Production System. *International Journal of Production Research, 45*(16), 3639–3664.

Blackwell, M., Iacus, S., King, G., & Porro, G. (2009). cem: Coarsened exact matching in Stata. *Stata Journal, 9*(4), 524.

Blank, S. (2013). *The Four Steps to the Epiphany*. K&S Ranch.

Bonazzi, F. (1993). *Il tubo di cristallo*. Il Mulino, Bologna.

Bonfiglioli Consulting (ed.) (2006). *Guardare Oltre: Pensare Snello Lean-Thinking (Più Produttività—Minori Sprechi) per Recuperare Competitività in Tutto il Sistema Italia.* Angeli, Milano.

Bonfiglioli, R. (2001). *Pensare Snello—Lean Thinking alla Maniera Italiana.* Franco Angeli, Milano.

Bou, J. C., & Beltran, I. (2005). Total quality management, high-commitment human resource strategy and firm performance: An empirical study. *Total Quality Management, 16*(1), 71–86.

Boyer, K. K. (1996). An assessment of managerial commitment to lean production. *International Journal of Operations & Production Management, 16*(9), 48–59.

Brown, K. L., & Inman, R. A. (1993). Small business and JIT: A managerial overview. *International Journal of Operations and Production Management, 13*(3), 57–66.

Browning, T., & Heath, R. (2009). Reconceptualizing the effects of lean on production costs with evidence from the F-22 program. *Journal of Operations Management, 27*, 23–44.

Buzzavo, L. (2008). Business strategies and key success factors for automotive retailers: The case of dealer groups in Italy. *International Journal of Automotive Technology and Management, 8*(1), 105–119.

Byrne, A. (2012). *The Lean Turnaround: How Business Leaders Use Lean Principles to Create Value and Transform Their Company.* McGraw-Hill Professional.

Campos, J., & Ballad, J.-C. (2009). *The Voice of the Customer for Product Development.* Multimedia, Oshawa, Canada.

Camuffo, A. (2004). Rolling out a world car: Globalization, outsourcing and modularity in the auto industry. *Korean Journal of Political Economy, 2*(1), 183–224.

Camuffo, A. (2014). *L'arte di Migliorare: Made in Lean Italy per Tornare a Competere.* Venezia, Marsilio Editori.

Camuffo, A., & Grandinetti, R. (2011). Italian industrial districts as cognitive systems: Are they still reproducible? *Entrepreneurship & Regional Development, 23*(9–10), 815–852.

Camuffo, A., & Massone, L. (2001). Relazioni industriali e globalizzazione: La strategia di Fiat Auto. *Economia & Management, 1*, 55–74.

Camuffo, A., & Micelli, S. (1997). Spain, France and Italy: Mediterranean lean production. In T. A. Kochan, R. D. Lansbury, & J. P. MacDuffie (eds.), *After Lean Production: Evolving Employment Practices in the World Auto Industry.* Cornell University Press, Ithaca, NY.

Camuffo, A., & Micelli, S. (1999). Teamwork and new forms of work organization in Fiat's integrated factory. In J. P. Durand, P. Stewart, & J. J. Castillo (eds.), *Teamwork in the Automobile Industry. Radical Change or Passing Fashion?* MacMillan Business, London.

Camuffo, A., & Secchi, R. (2016). Rolling out lean production systems: A knowledge-based perspective. *International Journal of Operations & Production Management, 36*(1), 61–85.

Camuffo, A., & Volpato, G. (1998). Making manufacturing lean in the Italian automobile industry: The trajectory of Fiat. In M. Freyssenet, A. Mair, K. Shimizu, & G. Volpato (eds.), *One Best Way? Trajectories and Industrial Models of the World's Automobile Producers.* Oxford University Press, New York.

Camuffo, A., & Volpato, G. (1997a). Building capabilities in assembly automation: Fiat experiences from Robogate to the Melfi plant. In K. Shimokawa, U. Juergens, & T. Fujimoto (eds.), *Transforming Automobile Assembly: Experience in Automation and Work Organization.* Berlin-Heidelberg, Springer-Verlag.

Camuffo, A., & Volpato, G. (1997b). Italy: Changing the workplace in the auto industry. In T. A. Kochan, R. D. Lansbury, & J. P. MacDuffie (eds.), *After Lean Production: Evolving Employment Practices in the World Auto Industry.* Cornell University Press, Ithaca, NY.

Camuffo, A., & Volpato, G. (1997c). *Nuove Forme di Integrazione Operativa: Il Caso Della Componentistica Automobilistica.* Franco Angeli, Milano.

Camuffo, A., & Volpato, G. (2002). Partnering in the global auto industry: The FIAT-GM strategic alliance. *International Journal of Automotive Technology and Management,* 2(3), 335–354.

Camuffo, A., De Stefano, F., & Paolino, C. (2015). Safety reloaded: Lean operations and high involvement work practices for sustainable workplaces. *Journal of Business Ethics,* 1–15.

Camuffo, A., & Gerli, F. (2016). The complex determinants of financial Results in a Lean Transformation process: The case of Italian SMEs. In *Complexity in Entrepreneurship, Innovation and Technology Research* (pp. 309–330). Springer International Publishing.

Cappellozza, F., Bruni, I., & Panizzolo, R. (2009). *Aumentare la Competitività attraverso la Lean Transformation. Casi di studio e applicazioni pratiche nel Nord-Est Italia* (pp. 16–30; 197–205). Este Editore, Milano.

Carrel, A. (1965). *Reflections on Life.* Hawthorn Books.

Carrieri, M., & Garibaldo, F. (1993). *Fiat Punto e a Capo: Problemi e Prospettive della Fabbrica Integrata da Termoli a Melfi.* Ediesse, Roma.

Cerruti, G., Ferigo, T., & Follis, M. (1996). *Produzione Snella e Professionalità: I Casi SKF e Zanussi Componenti Plastica.* Angeli, Milano.

Cerruti, G., & Rieser, V. (1991). *Fiat: Qualità Totale e Fabbrica Integrata.* Ediesse, Roma.

Chandler, G. N., & McEvoy, G. M. (2000). Human resource management, TQM, and firm performance in small and medium-size enterprises. *Entrepreneurship: Theory and Practice,* 25(1), 43–57.

Chiarini, A. (2012). Lean production: Mistakes and limitations of accounting systems inside the SME sector. *Journal of Manufacturing Technology Management,* 23(5), 681–700.

Claycomb, C., Germain, R., & Dröge, C. (1999). Total system JIT outcomes: Inventory, organization and financial effects. *International Journal of Physical Distribution & Logistics Management,* 29(10), 612–630.

Conterio, A., & Da Villa, F. (1995). The arsenal of the Venetian republic. In J. M. Juran (ed.), *A History of Managing for Quality, The Evolution, Trends, and the Future Directions of Managing for Quality* (pp. 301–347). Wisconsin, USA.

Cua, K. O., McKone, K. E., & Schroeder, R. G. (2001). Relationships between implementation of TQM, JIT, and TPM and manufacturing performance. *Journal of Operations Management,* 19(2), 675–694.

Danese, P., Romano, P., & Bortolotti, T. (2012). JIT production, JIT supply and performance: Investigating the moderating effects. *Industrial Management & Data Systems,* 112(3), 441–465.

Deming, E. W. (1986). *Out of the Crisis: Quality, Productivity and Competitive Position.* Cambridge University Press, Cambridge.

Dennis, P. (2006). *Getting the Right Things Done.* The Lean Enterprise Institute, Cambridge, MA.

Dennis, P. (2010). *The Remedy: Bringing Lean Thinking out of the Factory to Transform the Entire Organization.* John Wiley & Sons, New York.

De Toni, A., & Tonchia, S. (1996). Lean organization, management by process and performance measurement. *International Journal of Operations & Production Management,* 16(2), 221–236.

Dinero, D. (2005). *Training within Industry: The Foundation of Lean.* Productivity Press, New York.

Dweck, C. S. (2006). *Mindset.* Random House, New York.

Emiliani, B. (2008). *Practical Lean Leadership: A Strategic Leadership Guide for Executives.* Center for Lean Business Management, Kensington, CT.

Emiliani, B., Stec, D. J., Grasso, L., & Stodder, J. (2007). *Better Thinking, Better Results: Case Study and Analysis of an Enterprise-Wide Lean Transformation.* Center for Lean Business Management, Kensington, CT.

Emiliani, M. L. (1998). Lean behaviors. *Management Decision, 36*(9), 615–631.

Emiliani, M. L. (2000). Supporting small businesses in their transition to lean production. *Supply Chain Management: An International Journal, 5*(2), 66–71.

Emiliani, M. L. (2003). Linking leaders' beliefs to their behaviors and competencies. *Management Decision, 41*(9), 893–910.

Eroglu, C., & Hofer, C. (2011). Lean, leaner, too lean? The inventory-performance link revisited. *Journal of Operations Management, 29*(4), 356–369.

Flynn, B. B., Sakakibara, S., & Schroeder, R. G. (1995). Relationship between JIT and TQM: Practices and performance. *Academy of Management Journal, 38*(5), 1325–1360.

Forrester, J. W. (1964). *Industrial Dynamics.* MIT Press, Cambridge, MA.

Fortunato, V. (2008). *Ripensare la FIAT di Melfi: Condizioni di Lavoro e Relazioni Industriali Nell'era del World Class Manufacturing* (Vol. 28). Carocci.

Fortunato, V. (2012). *La Fiat e il lavoro operaio nella manifattura di classe mondiale. Sociologia del lavoro,* n. 126.

Fujimoto, T. (1999). *The evolution of a manufacturing system at Toyota.* Oxford University Press, New York.

Fullerton, R. R., & Wempe, W. F. (2009). Lean manufacturing, non-financial performance measures, and financial performance. *International Journal of Operations and Production Management, 29*(3), 212–240.

Fullerton, R. R., Kennedy, F. A., & Widener, S. K. (2014). Lean manufacturing and firm performance: The incremental contribution of lean management accounting practices. *Journal of Operations Management, 32*(7), 414–428.

Fullerton, R. R., McWatters, C. S., & Fawson, C. (2003). An examination of the relationship between JIT and financial performance. *Journal of Operations Management, 21*(4), 383–404.

Furlan, A., Dal Pont, G., & Vinelli, A. (2011a). On the complementarity between internal and external just-in-time bundles to build and sustain high performance manufacturing. *International Journal of Production Economics, 133*(2), 489–495.

Furlan, A., Vinelli, A., & Dal Pont, G. (2011b). Complementarity and lean manufacturing bundles: An empirical analysis. *International Journal of Operations & Production Management, 31*(8), 835–850.

Galgano, A. (1990). *La Qualità Totale. Il Company Wide Quality Control Come Nuovo Sistema Manageriale,* ed. Il Sole 24 Ore Libri.

Galgano, A. (2002). *Le Tre Rivoluzioni. Caccia Agli Sprechi: Raddoppiare La Produttività Con La Lean Production.* Guerini & Associati, Milano.

Galgano, A. (2005). *Toyota. Perchè l'industria Italiana non Progredisce.* Guerini e Associati, Milano.

Garrahan, P., & Stewart, P. (1992). *The Nissan Enigma: Flexibility at Work in a Local Economy.* Mansell, London.

George, M. L., Rowlands, D., & Kastle, B. (2004). *What Is Lean Six Sigma?* McGraw-Hill, New York.

Gittell, J. H. (2003). *The Southwest Airlines Way: Using the Power of Relationships to Achieve High Performance*. McGraw-Hill, New York.

Goldratt, E. M., & Cox, J. (1984). *The Goal: A Process of Ongoing Improvement*. North River Press.

Golicic, S. L., & Medland, S. (2007). Size might matter: A case study of lean implementation in an SME. *Society for Marketing Advances Proceedings*, 261–264.

Graupp, P., & Wrona, R. J. (2006). *The TWI Workbook. Essential Skills for Supervisors*. Productivity Press, New York.

Gualtieri, F. (1985). *Circoli della Qualità, Quaderni di Formazione*, n. 53, Edizioni Pirelli SpA, Milano.

Hines, P., & Rich, N. (1997). The seven value stream mapping tools. *International Journal of Operations & Production Management, 17*.

Hines, P., Found, P., Griffiths, G., & Harrison, R. (2011). *Staying Lean. Thriving, Not Just Surviving*. CRC Productivity Press, New York.

Hines, P., Silvi, R., & Bartolini, M. (2003). *From Lean to Profit*. Franco Angeli, Milano.

Hofer, C., Eroglu, C., & Hofer, A. R. (2012). The effect of lean production on financial performance: The mediating role of inventory leanness. *International Journal of Production Economics, 138*, 242–253.

Huson, M., & Nanda, D. (1995). The impact of just-in-time manufacturing on firm performance in the US. *Journal of Operations Management, 12*, 297–310.

Imai, M. (1995). *Gemba Kaizen: A Commonsense, Low-cost Approach to Management*. McGraw-Hill, New York.

Jackson, T. L. (2006). *Hoshin Kanri for the Lean Enterprise*. Productivity Press, New York.

Jayaram, J., Vickery, S., & Dröge, C. (2008). Relationship building, lean strategy and firm performance: An exploratory study in the automotive supplier industry. *International Journal of Production Research, 46*(20), 5633–5649.

Jones, D. T. (2006). Heijunka: Leveling production, *Manufacturing Engineering Magazine, 137*(2).

Jones, D. T., & Womack, J. P. (2011). *Seeing the Whole: Mapping the Extended Value Stream*. Lean Enterprise Institute, Cambridge, MA.

Juran, J., & De Feo, A. (2010). *Juran's Quality Handbook: The Complete Guide to Performance Excellence*. McGraw-Hill, New York.

Kaynak, H. (2003). The relationship between total quality management practices and their effects on firm performance. *Journal of Operations Management, 21*(4), 405–435.

Kennedy, F. A., & Widener, S. K. (2008). A control framework: Insights from evidence on lean accounting. *Management Accounting Research, 19*(4), 301–323.

Kenney, M., & Florida, R. (1991). Transplanted organisations: The transfer of Japanese industrial organisation to the U.S. *American Sociological Review, 56*, 381–398.

Keyte, B., & Locher, D. (2004). *The Complete Lean Enterprise: Value Stream Mapping for Administrative and Office Processes*. Productivity Press, New York.

Kinney, M. R., & Wempe, W. F. (2002). Further evidence on the extent and origins of JIT's profitability effects. *The Accounting Review, 77*(1), 203–225.

Koenigsaecker, G. (2009). *Leading the Lean Enterprise Transformation*. Productivity Press, New York.

Kogut, B., & Kulatilaka, N. (2001). Capabilities as real options. *Organization Science, 12*(6), 744–758.

Lane, G. (2007). *Made-to-Order Lean: Excelling in a High-Mix, Low-Volume Environment*. Productivity Press, New York.

Lanzara, G., & Patriotta, G. (2007). The institutionalization of knowledge in an automotive factory: Templates, inscriptions, and the problem of durability. *Organization Studies,* *28*(5), 635–660.

Lewis, M. A. (2000). Lean production and sustainable competitive advantage. *International Journal of Operations & Production Management, 20*(8), 959–978.

Liker, J. K. (2004). *The Toyota Way: 14 Management Principles from the World's Greatest Manufacturer.* McGraw-Hill, New York.

Liker, J. K., & Ballé, M. (2013). Lean managers must be teachers. *Journal of Enterprise Transformation, 3*(1), 16–32.

Liker, J. K., & Convis, G. R. (2012). *The Toyota Way to Lean Leadership: Achieving and Sustaining Excellence through Leadership Development.* McGraw-Hill, New York.

Liker, J. K., & Franz, J. K. (2011). *The Toyota Way to Continuous Improvement.* McGraw-Hill, New York.

Liker, J. K., & Hoseus, M. (2008). *Toyota Culture, The Heart & Soul of the Toyota Way.* McGraw-Hill, New York.

Liker, J. K., & Meier, D. P. (2007). *Toyota Talent: Developing Your People the Toyota Way.* McGraw-Hill, New York.

Locher, D. A. (2008). *Value Stream Mapping for Lean Development: A How-to Guide to Streamlining Time to Market.* Productivity Press, New York.

Losonci D., & Demeter K. (2013). Lean production and business performance: International empirical results. *Competitiveness Review, 23*(3), 218–233.

Lucey, J., Bateman, N., & Hines, P. (2005). Why major lean transitions have not been sustained. *Management Services, 49*(2), 9–13.

MacDuffie, J. P. (1995). Human resource bundles and manufacturing performance: Organizational logic and flexible production systems in the world auto industry. *Industrial and Labor Relations Review, 48*(2), 196–218.

Mackelprang, A. W., & Nair, A. (2010). Relationship between just-in-time manufacturing practices and performance: A meta-analytic investigation. *Journal of Operations Management, 28*, 283–302.

Maiga, A. S., & Jacobs, F. A. (2009). JIT performance effects: A research note. *Advances in Accounting, Incorporating Advances in International Accounting, 25*, 183–189.

Mann, D. (2014). *Creating a Lean Culture: Tools to Sustain Lean Conversions.* CRC Press, New York.

Martichenko, R., & Grabe, K. V. (2010). *Building a Lean Fulfillment Stream: Rethinking Your Supply Chain and Logistics to Create Maximum Value at Minimum Total Cost.* Lean Enterprise Institute, Cambridge, MA.

Maskell, B., & Baggaley, B. (2003). *Practical Lean Accounting.* Productivity Press, New York.

Maskell, B. H., & Kennedy, F. A. (2007). Why do we need lean accounting and how does it work? *Journal of Corporate Accounting and Finance, 18*, 59–73.

McGrath, R. G., & MacMillan, I. C. (2009). *Discovery-Driven Growth: A Breakthrough Process to Reduce Risk and Seize Opportunity.* Harvard Business School Press, Boston.

Merli, G. (1985). *I circoli della qualità.* Edizioni Lavoro, Roma.

Merli, G. (1991). *Total Quality Management. La Qualità Totale Come Strumento di Business.* ISEDI, Torino.

Mesut, Y., & Elif, A. (2007). Production smoothing in just-in-time manufacturing systems: A review of the models and solution approaches. *International Journal of Production Research, 45*(16), 3579–3597.

Mia, L. (2000). Just-in-time manufacturing, management accounting systems and profitability. *Accounting and Business Research, 30*(2), 137–151.

Monden, Y. (2012). *Toyota Production System: An Integrated Approach to Just-in-Time* (4th ed.). CRC Press, Boca Raton, FL.

Muller, E., & Zenker, A. (2001). Business services as actors of knowledge transformation: The role of KIBS in regional and national innovation systems. *Research Policy, 30*(9).

Ohno, T. (1988). *Toyota Production System: Beyond Large-Scale Production.* Productivity Press, Boston.

Pfeffer, J., & Sutton, R. I. (2000). *The Knowing-Doing Gap: How Smart Companies Turn Knowledge into Action.* Harvard Business School Press, Boston.

Pfeffer, J., & Sutton, R. I. (2006). *Hard Facts, Dangerous Half-Truths and Total Nonsense: Profiting from Evidence-Based Management.* Harvard Business School Press, Boston.

Pichierri, A. (1994). Produzione snella e ambiente locale. *Meridiana*, 179–193.

Porter, M. E. (1998). Clusters and the new economics of competition. *Harvard Business Review*, November–December.

Portioli-Staudacher, A., & Tantardini, M. (2012). Lean implementation in non–repetitive companies: A survey and analysis. *International Journal of Services and Operations Management, 11*(4), 385–406.

Powell, T. (1995). Total quality management as competitive advantage: A review and empirical study. *Strategic Management Journal, 16*, 15–37.

Pulignano, V. (1999). Gli effetti del teamwork sull'organizzazione sindacale alla Rover e alla Fiat. In M. Magnabosco & G. Sivini (eds.), *Oltre Melfi: La Fabbrica Integrata, Bilancio e Comparazioni* (pp. 35–50). Soveria Mannelli, Rubbettino.

Pulignano, V. (2000). Organizzazione snella e sindacato: Due stabilimenti europei a confronto. *Studi Organizzativi, 1*, 157–183.

Ries, E. (2011). *The Lean Startup: How Today's Entrepreneurs Use Continuous Innovation to Create Radically Successful Businesses.* Crown Books.

Rother, M. (2009). *Toyota Kata: Managing People for Improvement, Adaptiveness and Superior Results.* McGraw-Hill, New York.

Rother, M., & Harris, R. (2001). *Creating Continuous Flow.* Lean Enterprise Institute, Cambridge, MA.

Rother, M., & Shook, J. (1999). *Learning to See. Value Stream Mapping to Create Value and Eliminate Muda.* The Lean Enterprise Institute, Inc., Cambridge, MA.

Sakakibara, S., Flynn, B. B., Schroeder, R. G., & Morris, W. T. (1997). The impact of just-in-time manufacturing and its infrastructure on manufacturing performance. *Management Science, 43*(9), 1246–1257.

Sako, M. (2004). Supplier development at Honda, Nissan and Toyota: Comparative case studies of organizational capability enhancement. *Industrial and Corporate Change, 13*(2), 281–308.

Samson, D., & Terziovski, M. (1999). The relationship between total quality management practices and operational performance. *Journal of Operations Management, 17*(5), 393–409.

Schonberger, R. J. (1986). *World Class Manufacturing: The Lessons of Simplicity Applied.* Free Press, New York.

Seddon, J. (2005). *Freedom from Command & Control. Rethinking Management for Lean Service.* Productivity Press, New York.

Senge, P. (1990). *The Fifth Discipline: The Art and Practice of the Learning Organization.* Doubleday, New York.

Shah, R., & Ward, P. T. (2003). Lean manufacturing: Context, practice bundles, and performance. *Journal of Operations Management, 21*(2), 129–150.

Shah, R., & Ward, P. T. (2007). Defining and developing measures of lean production. *Journal of Operations Management, 25*, 785–805.

Shingo, S. (1983). *A Revolution in Manufacturing: The SMED System*. Productivity Press, Stanford, CA.

Shook, J. (2008). *Managing to Learn: Using the A3 Management Process to Solve Problems, Gain Agreement, Mentor, and Lead*. The Lean Enterprise Institute, Cambridge.

Smalley, A. (2004). *Creating Level Pull: A Lean Production-System Improvement Guide for Production-Control, Operations, and Engineering Professionals (Lean Tool Kit)*. Lean Enterprise Institute, Cambridge, MA.

Snee, R. D. (2006). The hard part: Holding gains in improvement: Sustaining the gains beings when the improvement initiative is launched not after the improvements are achieved. *Quality Progress*, September, 52–56.

Snee, R. D. (2010). Lean Six Sigma—Getting better all the time. *International Journal of Lean Six Sigma, 1*(1), 9–29.

Sobek, D. K., II, & Smalley, A. (2008). *Understanding A3 Thinking: A Critical Component of Toyota's PDCA Management System*. CRC Press, Boston.

Spear, S. (2004). Learning to lead at Toyota. *Harvard Business Review*, May, 78–86.

Spear, S., & Bowen, H. K. (1999). Decoding the DNA of the Toyota Production System. *Harvard Business Review, 77*(5), 96–106.

Stenzel, J. (2008). *Lean Accounting: Best Practices for Sustainable Integration*. Wiley, New York.

Sterman, J. D. (2000). *Business Dynamics: Systems Thinking and Modeling for a Complex World*. Irwin/McGraw-Hill.

Strambach, S. (2001). Innovation processes and the role of knowledge-intensive business services. In K. Koschatzky, M. Kulicke, & A. Zenker (eds.), *Innovation Networks. Concepts and Challenges in the European Perspective*. Physica, Heidelberg.

Sugimori, Y., Kusunoki, K., Cho, F., & Uchikawa, S. (1977). Toyota Production System and kanban system: Materialisation of just-in-time and respect-for-human system. *International Journal of Production Research, 15*(6), 553–564.

Szulanski, G., & Winter, S. (2002). Replication of organizational routines: Conceptualizing the exploitation of knowledge assets. In C. W. Choo & N. Bontis (eds.), *The Strategic Management of Intellectual Capital and Organizational Knowledge* (pp. 207–221). Oxford University Press, Oxford.

Trigeorgis, L. (1995). *Real Options in Capital Investment: Models, Strategies, and Applications*. Greenwood Publishing Group.

Tuccino, F. (2011). Il nuovo modello di organizzazione del lavoro in FIAT: Il sistema ergo-uas. Gli effetti sulla salute e sulle condizioni di lavoro. *Economia & Lavoro, 45*(2), 43.

Van Dun, D. H., & Wilderom, C. P. (2012). Human dynamics and enablers of effective lean team cultures and climates. *International Review of Industrial and Organizational Psychology, 27*, 115–152.

Van Landeghem, H., & April, J. (2010). People driven productivity: Lean for small businesses. 16th World Productivity Congress; 2010 European Productivity Conference: Productivity at crossroads: Creating a socially, economically and environmentally responsible world.

Volpato, G. (2004). *Fiat Auto. Crisi e Riorganizzazioni Strategiche di un'impresa Simbolo*. ISEDI, Torino.

Volpato, G. (2007). *Fiat Group Autombiles, un'araba Fenice Nell'industria Automobilistica Internazionale*. Il Mulino, Bologna.

Volpato, G. (2011). *Fiat Group Automobiles: le Nuove Sfide*. Il Mulino, Bologna.

War Production Board, Bureau of Training, Training Within Industry Service (1943). *Job Instruction: Sessions Outline and Reference Material*. US Government Printing Office.

Ward, A. C., & Sobek, D. K., II (2014). *Lean Product and Process Development*. Lean Enterprise Institute, Cambridge, MA.

White, R. E., Pearson, J. N., & Wilson, J. R. (1999). JIT manufacturing: A survey of implementation in small and large U.S. manufacturers. *Management Science, 45*(1), 1–15.

Womack, J. P. (2011). *Gemba Walks*. The Lean Enterprise Institute, Cambridge, MA.

Womack, J. P., & Jones, D. T. (1996). *Lean Thinking. Banish Waste and Create Wealth in Your Corporation*. Simon and Schuster, New York.

Womack, J. P., & Jones, D. T. (2005). Lean consumption. *Harvard Business Review, 83*(3), 58–68.

Womack, J., Jones, D. T., & Roos, D. (1990). *The Machine that Changed the World*. MacMillan Press, New York.

Yamashina, H. (1995). Japanese manufacturing strategy and the role of total productive maintenance. *Journal of Quality in Maintenance Engineering, 1*(1), 1355–1386.

Yamashina, H. (1996). Japanese manufacturing strategy—Competing with the tigers. *Business Strategy Review, 7*(2), 36.

Yamashina, H., & Kubo, T. (2002). Manufacturing cost deployment. *International Journal of Production Research, 40*(16), 4077–4091.

Yang, M. G., Hong, P., & Modi, S. B. (2011). Impact of lean manufacturing and environmental management on business performance: An empirical analysis of manufacturing firms. *International Journal of Production Economics, 129*, 251–261.

Index

Page numbers ending in "f" refer to figures. Page numbers ending in "t" refer to tables.